The Symbolism of the Pictish Stones

in Scotland

A Study of Origins

P. A. Jastrzębski

Scale of 1 Foot.

I.

AT BRODIE.

The Symbolism of the Pictish Stones

in Scotland

A Study of Origins

Inga Gilbert

Illustrations by
Frances Gilbert
or as otherwise credited in the List of Illustrations

Speedwell Books
Edinburgh and Dorchester

By the same author

Reflections on Paintings of Douglas Portway
A Kind of Madness – The Sculptures of Peter Eugene Ball

First published in 1995 by Speedwell Books
48 High West Street, Dorchester, Dorset DT1 1UT

Edited by David Gilbert and Stephanie Gilbert

Designed and typeset by Speedwell Books

Printed in Great Britain
by Henry Ling Limited, The Dorset Press
Dorchester DT1 1HD

A catalogue record for this book is available
from the British Library

ISBN 1 870068 03 3

Frontispiece: The Brodie Stone, a sepia wash drawing in
The Sculptured Stones of Scotland, Vol. I, 1856, by John Stuart

Contents

*It is through the language of archetypal symbols
that we reconnect ourselves with the primordial
ground from which all human culture has sprung
and through which we may discover our common
heritage.*

Lama Anagarika Govinda

Introduction

The title of this book could have been *The Elephant's Skin*. The image of a 'floating' elephant has been one of the many mysterious symbols of Pictish art. Many books have been written about the Picts and the possible meaning of their signs; but we have so far held the wrong keys to a better understanding of Pictish symbols. Yet Pictish art speaks a very precise language. The symbols on the old stones had clear meaning and related to what must once have been well-known stories. We have therefore to search for a new way of deciphering this symbolic language. The key to one image may prove to be the master key to all the others. The elephant's skin is such an image.

It would, however, be misleading to present the reader with the interpretation of one sign out of context. We shall therefore choose a different approach, more laborious without doubt, for we have to travel back in history and retrace steps which lead back to origins. In our journey we shall see many places and civilizations rising up like phantoms out of the past. They have all disappeared under sand, earth and water but we will try and collect some of the stones which are still standing and see in them 'words' and 'meaning' until we come somewhat nearer to the understanding and appreciation of an ancient people and their culture.

The Picts seem to be lost in the mists of time. They were known and feared as fierce warriors who menaced the Romans as the Caledonii and related tribes from the time the first Roman legions reached the area of the river Tay in about 79 AD. The word *Picti* might be a name given by the Romans to their northern adversaries, referring to painted or tattooed marks and meaning 'the painted ones'. *Picti* could equally be a latinized version of a native name.

In the first century BC the historian Diodorus Siculus reports that a Greek voyager called Pytheas sailed around Britain about 325 BC. Pytheas is said to have stated that the British Isles were called the Pretanic Islands. This name eventually had come to be applied to the people of the whole of Britain and during the Roman period the natives of southern Britain called themselves the Pritani or Brittones. The northern population probably used the form Priteni. The name is presumably Celtic and may mean 'the people of the designs'. The old Irish derivates of Priteni are Cruithin and Cruithni. The name Priteni, applied to the people north of the Antonine Wall, eventually came to mean the 'Picts'.

The first known recorded mention of *Picti* is in a panegyric by Eumenius of 297 AD. By the fourth century AD we learn from Ammianus Marcellinus that the Picts were divided into northern and southern peoples.

The language spoken by the Picts may have been what philologists call P-Celtic. 'The *Common Celtic* branch of the parent Indo-European stem is divided into two great families, *Q-Celtic* and *P-Celtic*. The most important of a number of distinguishing marks of Q-Celtic is the fact that it preserves the original Indo-European *qu* unaltered; and one of the chief characteristics of P-Celtic is that it turned this *qu* into *p* , a change which took place also in some Greek and Italic dialects.'[1] As the P-Celtic language of Scotland had some affinity with Gaulish, we can also speak of a Gallo-Brittonic language current in northern Scotland before the fifth century AD, when Scotland was invaded by Irish Gaels whose language would have been Q-Celtic.

But the Picts also spoke another language which so far we have been unable to trace and which was not an Indo-European language. We know that St. Columba, who came from Ireland and is said to have converted the northern Picts to Christianity in the sixth century, had to make use of an interpreter[2] in conversing with the Picts. It is a question of argument whether a mere difference of dialect between the Irish and the northern Picts would have warranted the use of an interpreter.

The best information about the Picts comes to us through the 'father' of English history and church chronicles, the Venerable Bede, *Baeda Venerabilis,* the Benedictine who wrote in the eighth century. His monastery of Jarrow had been in very close contact with the Picts during his lifetime. Bede says that ' At the present time there are in Britain ... five languages and four nations — English (the Angles), British (the Brittonic people), Irish (the Gaelic people) and Picts. Each of these have their own language: but all are united in their study of God's truth by the fifth — Latin

— which has become a common medium through the study of the scriptures.' [3]

Bede clearly implies that in his day the Picts spoke a language which was distinct both from Gaelic and Brittonic, a language which was non-Celtic. The high proportion of non-Celtic tribe and place names in Pictland is remarkable, as Ptolemy's map of Roman Scotland shows. His toponomy of northern Scotland was drawn up at the end of the first century AD. Many names of towns, rivers, bays, capes and islands north of the Antonine Wall in the eastern parts extending to the Moray Firth derive from an unknown language, and some with sound changes still survive in our days. 'There were at least two languages current in northern Scotland before the coming of the Irish Gaels in the fifth century. One of them was a Gallo-Brittonic dialect not identical with the British spoken south of the Antonine Wall, though related to it. The other was not Celtic at all, nor apparently even Indo-European, but was presumably the speech of some very early set of inhabitants of Scotland.' [4]

Historians have suggested various dates during which this non-Indo-European language could have been introduced into northern Scotland, and the general agreement suggests that it was a pre-Celtic language spoken by Bronze Age people. It seems to have survived until the last days of the Pictish nation. Ogam writing, an Irish invention introduced into Scotland in the fifth century AD and again, in a more evolved form in the eighth century, made use of this unknown language in the inscriptions added to the older symbol stones. Although Ogam is readable it is entirely unintelligible.

* * *

Early Celtic people of central Europe can be traced back to the last quarter of the second millennium BC. The descendants of this proto-Celtic society were the people of the Hallstatt culture, which, in broad terms, lasted from 750 to 450 BC. Hallstatt is a cemetery with over one thousand graves discovered in 1846 above the town of Hallstatt in the Salzbergtal in Upper Austria. Together with their successors from about 450 BC, the people of the La Tène culture, so named after a site at the northern-most tip of Lake Neuchâtel in Switzerland discovered in 1857, they represent the iron-using Celts of Europe, named the *Keltoi*, the *Galli* and *Galati* by classical writers. There is a hypothesis that Hallstatt elements could have penetrated from southern England as far as Scotland in the fifth or sixth century BC. The following La Tène culture, overlaying the Hallstatt elements, became the civilization of the Brittones and, archaeologically speaking, 'Pictish Celtic might be regarded as a P-Celtic dialect of Hallstatt antecedents and Brittonic as once primarily of La Tène antecedents.' [5]

In his *Ecclesiastical History* Bede states that 'Picts from Scythia put to sea in a few longships, and were driven by storms around the coasts of Britain, arriving at length on the north coast of Ireland,' then 'crossed into Britain, and began to settle in the north of the island.' [6] Celtic art, La Tène in particular, has always been shown to contain amongst Greek patterns and motifs, 'eastern "animal" art, primarily that of Scythian and other peoples in the area of Greek settlement on the shores of the Black Sea.' [7] Bede's statement, however, that the Picts came from Scythia has not been accepted by modern historians who have treated it as an invention, an error or, at best, as a legend. It has been suggested that instead of 'Scythia' we should read 'Scandia' or 'Scandinavia'. [8]

Present-day historians have persistently given a Christian character to Pictish art, following the Victorian writers such as J. Anderson. [9] We are thus taught to see biblical events in every Pictish narrative scene. Most interpretations which do not refer to battle or hunting scenes limit themselves to hinting at Adam and Eve and Jonah and the Whale, or referring to David and Daniel with lions. 'David rending the jaws of a lion' is a common theme and so is Daniel in the lions' den, and animals are always likened to the symbols of the Evangelists.

The Illuminations of early manuscripts such as the *Manuscript of the Cathedral Library of Durham, The Book of Durrow, The Lindisfarne Gospels* and *The Book of Kells* have been seen as a source of inspiration for the carvings on Pictish stones. The images in these Gospel books of interlaced bands and ribbons, spiral and border designs and rich ornamentation point to an eastern Mediterranean school of which Syrian, Mesopotamian and Egyptian elements lay claim to archaic traditions. But apart from the difficulties arising from the comparison of the art of two different media — that of Gospel illustration with that of stone carving — the conclusions are not convincing. We have only to think of the intricate design on bronzes and on work in gold by the European

Celts from the 5th century BC onwards to realize that no Gospel books were needed to set the pattern. It would be more appropriate to see in the styles of both similar origins, based on metal-work, rather than accept the theory that Pictish cross-slabs were inspired by early Irish or Northumbrian manuscript illuminations.

* * *

Until the 1960s European prehistorians had seen Mesopotamia as the Cradle of Civilization and the Fertile Crescent[10] as the source of agricultural innovations and of community life which extended its influence into Europe. Radiocarbon dating of organic matter has since tended to weaken the rôle played by the East: the European world emerges as more independent, more original and self-reliant. It is in this sense that we may understand new directions in historic appreciation: an insistence on immediate values taken *in situ*, on the spot, so to speak. But this emphasis on local and 'national' values tends to favour a disregard for 'genesis' and certainly keeps the Picts well at home. A few quotations may illustrate this point.

N. K. Sanders: '. . .we were formerly given to find all causes of major change in prehistoric societies in the movements of people from one region to another, by way either of invasion or migration, whereas now we prefer exploring the possibilities of indigenous evolution.'[11]

'. . .whereas in the Upper Palaeolithic we are looking at an art that is relevant to the wider history of man and the world, later on interest contracts to a purely European scale, until with the La Tène art of the last centuries BC we meet something that is very new, very individual, and completely European.'[12]

J. D. Mackie: 'In short, the Picts were an amalgam of peoples . . . and there is no doubt that they were the original inhabitants of the land.' To Mackie these original inhabitants produced a native art, which had come under foreign influence: 'Pictish art, in its developed form, drew on a stock of forms and symbols which was cosmopolitan, being influenced by both Anglian and Celtic traditions.'[13]

A. Ritchie: 'The Picts were not a new element in the population. They were simply descendants of indigenous iron-age tribes given a new name. From various references in the works of Roman authors, it appears that a process of tribal amalgamation took place during the Roman period . . .' [14]

C. Renfrew: '. . . we should look in each area for its own roots — unless we have clear reason to do otherwise.' [15]

Historical evaluation of 'indigenous evolution' and its emphasis on an immediate appreciation of the style at hand may open our eyes to artistic values. But the complete or partial disregard of roots beyond those found *in situ* will certainly impede further studies. We will learn little about the underlying thought or the origin of a people. Following such a theory, we are bound to confuse traditional values carried along by migrating people with new values evolved after settlement. This is a problem which has often troubled historians, particularly when origins are faint, and which N. K. Sanders sums up when referring to the outstanding work on *Early Celtic Art* by P. Jacobsthal: 'Jacobsthal admitted a problem and only partially resolved it when he said that Celtic art had three roots: the classical art of the Mediterranean, an eastern art meaning principally Scythia but in some ill-defined way Persia as well, and "native" meaning Hallstatt geometric art.' [16] A few quotations from Jacobsthal will take this point a little further: 'Celtic animal and mask styles are of oriental origin.' 'Some motives have their only analogies not in the arts of Scythia proper but in the Altai Mountains, Siberia and China: a fact that denies explanation.' 'Scythian art extended as far as China, while in Europe it influenced Celtic art and even left its mark, as it seems, on the Dark Age styles of the Migration period.' [17] Not much notice has been taken of Jacobsthal's theories by historians and his views tend to be brushed aside. Yet long before, John Stuart, in his *Sculptured Stones of Scotland*, volume second, Edinburgh 1867, had written: '. . . It seems impossible to explain the appearance of a Phoenician or Asiatic influence among the Pictish people of Scotland.' [18] The indications of Eastern influences observed by Jacobsthal, Stuart and others [19] have not been followed up, and the reluctance of western scholars to admit such influences in European art and thought has limited historical research and evaluation.

The French scholar, Georges Dumézil, saw a great continuity of Indo-European political and religious ideology from its extreme eastern boundaries in India to the extreme west in Ireland. He noticed that certain religious traditions were common to Brahmins and Druids. [20] He saw confirmation 'in the fact that, as the French scholar

J. Vendryes had shown, the Celtic languages, in common with Italic and Indo-Iranian, retain many elements of an old Indo-European terminology relating to religious belief and ritual.' [21]

A common Indo-European political and religious ideology in such far-off places as India and Ireland is for Colin Renfrew inconsistent with his view of prehistory, argued in his *Archaeology and Language*, that proto-Indo-Europeans had already started to move apart as early as around 7000 BC. Renfrew seeks to explain the similarities in social and religious structures as 'parallel evolution or 'coincidences'.[22] However, Dumézil's exhaustive studies and conclusions cannot be ignored, and they continue to receive substantial support from those who, to quote J. G. Mallory, 'maintain that the trifunctional ideology of the Proto-Indo-Europeans permeates the religious texts of the ancient Indians and Iranians, emerges in the epic poetry and drama of the Greeks, hides behind the façade of history among the early Romans, and expresses itself in the prose tales of the medieval Germanic and Celtic peoples'. [23]

* * *

The secret of the Pictish stones has been much debated, yet never solved. [24] The symbol stones are considered to be 'vivid works of art' [25] and the symbols themselves are mostly, according to present knowledge, unique in Europe. These monuments, once cult objects, now seem to loom like apparitions out of a dense mist. A few are still standing on or near their original sites, upright stones by the roadside, in fields, on hilltops, near churches. They are of local sandstone, granite, slate or whinstone. Some have been re–used by builders and put to other purposes in chapel walls, paved areas, graveyards and secular buildings. They are badly weathered and many have been re-trimmed or reconstructed, even damaged by cleaning; some are safely housed in museums. The stones are found in the heart of Pictland which extended on the eastern side of Scotland from the Firth of Forth to the Moray Firth, and they have also been found as far north as Orkney and Shetland.

Pictish stones reveal three distinctive styles: a decorative style, in relief, incorporating animals, plants and the Christian cross; a narrative style, telling historical or legendary events, also in relief; and an abstracted style showing symbolic incised signs. Heathen symbols on one side of a slab are often combined with a Christian cross on the other side; and earlier monuments were often re-used and Christian reliefs added to older, incised symbol stones. In some cases the symbols were added to the cross. We have an interesting example of a stone bearing 'cup-marks', such as are found upon standing stones of the Bronze Age (approximately 2000-500 BC), as well as pagan enigmatic symbols of a possibly later date, and Christian symbols.[26]

No doubt the mysterious relief carvings and incisions transmit a certain charm, they invite a certain *réverie* and tantalize the imagination. The dominant impression is that of great persistency on the part of the artists. We register that from pagan to Christian times the same symbols have been carefully repeated. Whatever these signs may mean, they have been executed in a clear style, there are no superfluous lines, no doubts about intentions, no question that what we cannot read has always been emphasised in the same precise language. This unfledging devotion to certain ideas and images which constantly recur should be encouraging in our quest and indeed be a clue to the unravelling of their past history.

* * *

The first writer to catalogue the Pictish stones was John Stuart, who produced two volumes magnificently illustrated in sepia wash, *Sculptured Stones of Scotland*, Vol. 1, 1856 (Aberdeen) and Vol. 2, 1867 (Edinburgh). This work included not only Pictish stones but other stones from Scotland and the English border counties. It was left to Joseph Anderson to single out early Celtic work and write his classic study of Pictish stones, *Scotland in Early Christian Times*, second series, the Rhind Lectures in Archaelogy for 1880.

Joseph Anderson remains by far the most thoughtful and original writer on the subject. He defined the Celtic area under Pictish influence as lying along the east side of Scotland, north of the Forth, from Fife to Caithness and reaching beyond to the Orkney and Shetland isles. He classified the Pictish stones as belonging to 'two types: the first and earlier type an erect slab, undressed to shape, and simply incised with symbols and figure-subjects; the second type also an erect slab, but shaped to a regular form, bearing on the obverse the cross of Celtic form, elaborately ornamented with interlaced work, spirals, and fretwork, and on the reverse the same symbols which are characteristic of the first type, but with higher art and a greater variety of figure-subjects.' [27]

In addition Anderson mentions two other types in the West of Scotland: 'the earlier type a free-standing cross of Celtic form, ornamented like the erect slabs in a pure style of Celtic art, but differing from them in the absence of the symbols; the later type also a free-standing cross, but not of Celtic form, ornamented with foliageous scrolls, and differing from all the earlier types in its bearing usually the representation of the crucifixion.' [28]

'But besides the monuments thus classified under the types that are prevalent in the eastern and western districts of Scotland respectively, there are other groups of less frequent occurrence, which present variations of such a nature as to prevent their being included in any general type.' [29]

Anderson's careful survey was further elaborated and systematized in *The Early Christian Monuments of Scotland*, 1903, by Joseph Anderson and Romilly Allen.[30] Allen combined Stuart's catalogue with analyses of subsequently discovered stones and with Anderson's findings. Anderson himself simplified his categories as follows:

1. Monuments with incised symbols only.
2. Monuments with symbols and Celtic ornament carved in relief.
3. Monuments with Celtic ornament in relief, but without the symbols of the other two classes.

This classification, which again is treated as chronological, has been adopted — as Classes I, II and III — in most subsequent writings on the subject.

Anderson confined Pictish stones as belonging to a period extending from the 7th to the 12th centuries AD. He greatly influenced all further research when he insisted that the symbols which appeared with the image of the cross had by necessity to be of a purely Christian character. [31] He argued that pictorial representations were taken from Scripture stories, 'intermingled with the grotesque and fabulous forms of the Divine Bestiaries or the common allegorical subjects, like the chase of the stag which pervaded the literature and art of the early Middle Ages.' [32]

Anderson thus relied on Christian teachers from a very early period, who catalogued 'beasts, birds, plants and minerals, that were symbolic of Christian virtues and doctrines.' [33] But, when writing about 'a national system of art like this of the Scottish monuments', he admitted that 'it does not necessarily follow that its essential elements must have originated in Scotland or in Ireland.' 'Some of these are common to a much wider area than that of Celtic Britain, or even of Europe.' [34]

Since the time of Joseph Anderson no convincing explanation of the Scottish symbol stones has yet come forward.[35] We shall therefore venture further afield and return to Bede, whose neglected statement that the Picts came from Scythia is our first signpost on our journey abroad.

NOTES TO INTRODUCTION

The quotation facing page 9 from Lama Anagarika Govinda is from his *Psycho-cosmic Symbolism of the Buddhist Stupa*, Dharma Publishing, California, 1976, Introduction, xvi

1   K. H. Jackson, 'The Pictish Language', Ch. VI, *The Problem of the Picts*, ed. F. T. Wainwright, London, 1955, pp. 129-130

2   Adamnan, *Life of St. Columba*, completed between AD 692 and 697

3   Bede, *Ecclesiastical History of the English People*, I. 1., transl. L. Sherley-Price, London, 1990, p. 45

4   K. H. Jackson, *op. cit.*, p. 152

5   Jackson, *ibid*, p. 156

6   Bede, *op. cit.*, p. 45-46

7   Sir Cyril Fox, *Pattern and Purpose*, Cardiff, 1958, p. xxi

8   J. M. Wallace-Hadrill, *Bede's Ecclesiastical History —
    A Historical Commentary*, Oxford, 1988, and Bede, *op. cit.*, p. 45, footnote 2

9   J. Anderson, *Scotland in Early Christian Times*, Edinburgh, 1881

10 The Fertile Crescent stretches from Israel and Jordan to northern Iraq and western Iran, down to the Persian Gulf (spreading to areas in south-east Anatolia).

11 N. K. Sanders, *Prehistoric Art in Europe*, 2nd. ed. London, 1985, Foreword to the Second Edition, p. 12

12 N. K. Sanders, *ibid*, Foreword to the First Edition, p. 10

13 J. D. Mackie, *A History of Scotland*, 2nd. ed. London, 1978, pp.16 and 23

14 A. Ritchie, *Picts*, Edinburgh, 1989, p. 6

15 C. Renfrew, *Archaeology and Language*, London, 1987, 1989, p. 175

16 N. K. Sanders, *op. cit.*, p. 344

17 P. Jacobsthal, *Early Celtic Art*, Oxford, 1944, reprint 1969, pp. 156, 158 and 163

18 Preface, p. 33

19 E.g. J. Strzygowski, *Die Baukunst der Armenier und Europa*, Vienna, 1918, Vol. 2, p. 712: 'Die dauernd auf das Mittelmeer allein gerichtete humanistische Vorbildung hat uns blind gemacht für

die Fragen des Weltverkehres.'

20 G. Dumézil, *L'idéologie tripartie des Indo-Européens*, Brussels, 1958, p. 11

21 P. MacCana, 'Celtic Religion and Mythology', *The Celts*, catalogue of exhibition in Palazzo Grassi, Venice, 1991, p. 603

22 C. Renfrew, *op. cit.*, esp. pp. 8, 146–150, 168, 251–253. Professor Renfrew's arguments have been convincingly challenged by Dr.J P. Mallory in his book mentioned in the following note 23

23 J. P. Mallory, *In Search of the Indo-Europeans*, London, 1989, p. 270

24 Explanations which have been suggested by different writers: 'personal memorials', 'funerary monuments', 'territorial markers', 'affirmations of the Christian faith', 'repetition on tombstones of tattooing marks', 'proclamations of marriage alliances between different lineages', 'a national flag'!

25 R. B. K. Stevenson, 'Pictish Art', Ch. V, *The Problem of the Picts* op. cit., p. 97

26 Meigle Museum, Perthshire, *Catalogue of Early Medieval Monuments*, exhibit no. 1

27 J. Anderson, *op. cit.*, p. 84

28 *Ibid*, p. 84

29 *Ibid.* Anderson mentions here that 'Perhaps the most singular of these is the Burghead group' of figures of bulls incised on small, rough, undressed stones.

30 Part I comprises Anderson's introduction, being the text of his Rhind lectures for 1892. Part II is Allen's archaeological survey, with his analyses, drawings and photographs.

31 J. Anderson, *op. cit*, p. 188

32 *Ibid*, p. 189

33 *Ibid*, p. 171, note 1

34 *Ibid*, p. 111

35 This is evident from the most recent study which discusses all the existing research and views, Elizabeth Sutherland's *In Search of the Picts* , London, 1994

* * *

PART I

Migrations, Myths and Magic

Chapter 1

Indo-European Ancestors

The Picts known to the Romans spoke a type of Celtic, possibly a language or dialect from the branch philologists now call P–Celtic. Little of the Pictish vocabulary is recorded, but we know that the Picts also retained non–Indo–European elements in their language. Celtic intrusion into Britain and Ireland is generally believed to have taken place during the 1st millennium BC, although some scholars prefer an earlier date. The Celtic language is an Indo–European language and we cannot discuss the Picts before tracing, in very broad terms, an outline of early Indo–European history.

Celtic communities were formed by many tribes and the definition of what is Celtic has to be based on linguistic, archaeological and stylistic studies. The current state of research into Celtic and Indo–European origins is still unresolved but a very convincing explanation, accepted by many linguists and archaeologists, is that by the middle of the fifth millennium BC Proto-Indo-European speaking people were settled in the steppe and forest steppe of the southern Ukraine and south Russia. The introduction of stock breeding, the domestication of the horse and the use of wheeled vehicles encouraged migration, and already during the late fourth millennium BC mobile societies of hunter–gatherers and pastoral nomads set out from Pontic-Caspian regions and travelled across the Eurasian steppe lands to the east, as far as the area of the river Yenisey and the Altai regions of southern Siberia.

We may assume that by the end of the Eneolithic period, about 3500-2500 BC, Indo–European speaking people emerged from Pontic-Caspian homelands.[1] Further expansions east and south-east took place, into today's Kazakhstan, Uzbekistan and Tadzhikistan. Another drift led further south through Central Asian communities into Afghanistan, North Pakistan and the Indus Valley. By 2000 BC Indo-Aryan (Indic) was spoken by the tribes south of the Caspian and we may conclude that Bronze Age Indo-Europeans of the steppe lands had evolved into the Indo-Iranians who conquered north-west India and the Punjab. A branch of these eastern Iranian people from the steppe lands also moved further west into present-day Iran and beyond into northern Syria. Historical linguists believe the individual Indic (or Indo-Aryan) and Iranian languages began to diverge by 2000 BC. The term Indo-Iranian is also used by scholars to identify Bronze Age steppe cultures of Central Asia and south Siberia which were the linear ancestors of eastern Iranians and Indo-Aryans. [2]

Pontic-Caspian communities also spread out into Northern and Central Europe and occupied a vast area extending from the upper Volga and the middle Dnieper to the Baltic, Holland and Switzerland. It is much debated how far the Corded Ware pottery of 3200—2300 BC indicated Pontic relationship to Northern and Central Europe.

By the third millennium BC Indo-European invasions of Anatolia had taken place and it is still not clear whether the Indo-European tribes reached Asia Minor from the north-west over the Balkans or by a south-eastern route from the Pontic steppe over the Caucasus. Continual movement of people from the steppe into south-eastern Europe took place and Early Bronze Age cultures reached southern Europe from northern Anatolia and from the Balkans via the Danubian basin.

We may call the Celts the most western of the Indo-European tribes. Scholars now agree that the formation of the Celtic language must have taken place in the second millennium BC, stretching from the Carpathian mountains west to Britain and Ireland and south to the Atlantic. Historical Celts first emerge for us in the archaeological finds of Hallstatt in Austria (ca 750-450 BC) and its continuation in the following La Tène culture in Switzerland (ca 450 BC until the first century AD). Hallstatt and La Tène are thus our main base for tracing Celtic identity, but Celtic origins are somewhat speculative and the perennial problem of how such concentrated cultural communities came into being is still with us. Some historians suggest that Celtic art received its main inspiration from ancient classical motifs and Mediterranean sources.[3] But the Mediterranean legacy must in fact be a very late one. Celtic migrations carried La Tène elements into Italy, invaded Greece and colonized central Anatolia, but if we take a closer look at Vedic beliefs and Indo-Iranian mythologies, at bronzes of the 8th and 7th centuries BC from bronze working centres such as Urartu and Luristan, then we must come to the conclusion that the Indo-European Celts had an earlier inheritance

1, 2   passed on to them from former eastern homelands. The Celts did not depend on later Mediterranean influences, even where such influences have been recognized when by way of trade and conquest new confrontations with older cultural links were established.

1 Part of a golden belt
   from Ziwiyeh, Iran

2 Piece of a Celtic bronze mount
   from Brno, Moravia

Celtic 'foreign' and therefore 'barbarian' elements survived in Europe parallel to sophisticated Greek and Roman traditions. But where Rome propagated a dry theology the Celtic world had retained a 'nature religion'. Moreover, Greek and Roman myths must also be understood with an ancient eastern legacy in mind.[4] When the early ethnographer Julius Caesar explained the Celtic gods by their Roman counterparts he was interpreting traditions inherited from earlier Indo-European mythologies.[5] There are striking parallels in the ideologies of the Indo-European and the Indo-Iranian worlds. The two limits of the Indo-European area — the eastern boundaries of India and the western shores of Ireland — maintain a vocabulary related to social and religious attitudes and behaviour which would be inconceivable without common antecedents in prehistoric thought. Although less clearly than in Roman myths, Celtic social realities indicate such a structure of ideological similarities. Irish myths reflect such a complex system, but they have come down to us filtered through the selective transcriptions of Christian scribes; gods, heroes and fairy people often merge into the same legendary personalities and interpretations of the myths are fraught with difficulties.[6]

Chapter 2

Pictorum de Scythia

Early Irish stories collected in later manuscripts provide us with unique evidence of Celtic myths. Unfortunately, by the time these stories were being written down, not before the 7th century AD, the original meanings of the oral traditions were being reworked and had already changed considerably by the 12th century AD, the earliest time from which any manuscripts survive. We learn very little about Irish religion. Indeed, Irish myths as they have come down to us are very similar in their intricate and lively style to Insular La Tène elements found in Irish art: decorative, rich in imagination, full of tension, but somehow never quite making sense and seemingly lacking in depth. In both cases the real meaning has been lost in an overwhelming stylization and we have to search through a bewildering mosaic of metamorphoses and fantasies before attempting to reconstruct any facts which might bear on the mythological and social history of the Celtic world.

An historical link between the Irish and the Picts is established for us in the *Ecclesiastical History* written in about 731 AD by the scholar monk Bede who lived most of his life at Jarrow: '. . . It is said that some Picts from Scythia (*Pictorum de Scythia*) put to sea in a few longships, and were driven by storms around the coast of Britain, arriving at length on the north coast of Ireland. Here they found the nation of the Irish, from whom they asked permission to settle; but their request was refused . . . These Pictish seafarers, as I have said, asked for a grant of land so that they could make a settlement. The Irish replied that there was not room for them both, but said: "We can give you good advice. We know that there is another island not far to the east, which we often see in the distance on clear days. If you choose to go there, you can make it fit to live in; should you meet resistance, we will come to your help." So the Picts crossed into Britain, and began to settle in the north of the island, since the Britons were in possession of the south. Having no women with them, these Picts asked for wives of the Irish, who consented on condition that, when any dispute arose, they should choose a king from the female royal line rather than the male. This custom continues among the Picts to this day . . .'[7] Bede's reference to Scythia, in the Pontic-Caspian steppe lands, as a place of origin has been questioned by historians for a long time and has often been ridiculed. Yet Scythia is mentioned in Irish myths and long journeys did not seem to have daunted the heroes of old.

In the story of Bricriu's Feast three chieftains — one of them is Cú Chulainn — contend amongst each other for the champion's portion. They travel to the stronghold of king Cú Rui who is to give the final judgement. There they are welcomed by Cú Rui's wife for 'Cú Ruí himself was not there that night, but he had . . . instructed his wife what to do with the heroes until he returned from Scythia.'[8] The same Cú Rui later assumes the guise of a giant in order to test the courage and the honour of Cú Chulainn and the other heroes. Before challenging the warriors he announces that 'That which I have come to seek I have not found in Ériu or the Alps or Europe or Africa or Greece or Scythia or Inis Orc or the Pillars of Hercules or Tor mBregoind or Inis Gaid. Nowhere have I found a man to keep my bargain.'[9] In the story of the Cattle Raid of Fróech two heroes, Conall and Fróech, also travel to distant places. 'They set out across the sea, across northern England and the Channel to northern Lombardy, until they reached the Alps.'[10] There they manage to retrieve the wife, the three sons and the cattle of Fróech who had all been abducted and become the property of a king who resided in a fort in the Alps.

Geoffrey of Monmouth mentions in his *Historia Regum Britanniae*, of ca 1136, (IV, 17), that the Picts came from Scythia with a great fleet and ravaged part of Scotland. The king of the Picts, Sodric, was killed in battle by the Britons but the Picts were allowed to live in Caithness. They asked for wives from the Britons and were rejected. The Picts then went to Ireland with the same request and were successful. This version by Geoffrey of Monmouth may possibly be treated as a secondary compilation of earlier Irish or Welsh sources. Geoffrey places this event some years after the Roman invasion of Britain under Claudius in 43 AD. It may have been just one of many Pictish invasions from Scythia. In his *Historia* Geoffrey of Monmouth is known to have combined what seems to be a well ordered chronicle with extravagant and imaginative stories, and the accuracy of his historical references has often been doubted. Yet another episode connecting Picts and Scythia takes place about 100 years later when the British leader Sulgenius 'crossed the sea to Scythia, hoping to be restored to power with the help of the Picts' (V, 2).

Five distinct Irish versions (dating from not earlier than the ninth century) of the story of Pictish invasions exist: [11]

1. A poem by Mael Mura: the Cruithni stole the women of Ireland. ' . . . In the old Irish period Cruithin and Cruithni have two senses; one the historical Picts, and the other, in regular use down to the eighth century, those people apparently of British immigrant stock in Ireland. As scholars have repeatedly pointed out, the latter were not Picts . . . ' [12]

2. The *History of the Descendants of Ír*: 36 soldiers from Thracia joined an expedition of the sons of Míl in Germany. (The Indo-European speaking Thracians who occupied the eastern half of the Balkans were neighbours of the Scythian tribes of the Mare Pontus.)

3. The *Book of Fermoy* : after expulsion from Ireland the Cruithni asked for wives.

4. The *Lebor Gabála Érenn*, the Book of Invasions: Cruithni from Thracia came to Ireland and received the widows of drowned Irish warriors.

5. The *Lebor Bretnach* : Cruithni first settled in Orkney, thence they moved to North Britain.

These references already indicate that travel over long distances was accepted as a normal occurrence. The Venerable Bede has always been esteemed as a fine historian and so let us trust him in this, as we do in other historical matters, and start our investigation with the Scythians.

Chapter 3

The Scythians

The Scythians were horse-mounted nomads who may have entered the area north of the Black Sea at the beginning of the first millennium BC. They could have come from an area east of the Volga. This theory however has been found to be somewhat unconvincing and historians tend to see the original homeland of the Scythians in the steppe regions of the Turanian Plain, Turkestan, or even in Siberia.[13]

The Scythians were of Indo-Iranian origin. From oriental and Greek sources we know that these *ashkuza* or *ishkuza*, menaced by another Iranian tribe, the Massagetae, towards the middle or the end of the 8th century BC, entered what is today Turkmenistan and travelled along the south coast of the Caspian Sea. Turning north they crossed over the river Araxes (Araks), leaving the Caucasus on their left. Moving north-west they approached the steppe land of southern Russia, the area north of the Mare Pontus, as the Black Sea was called in antiquity. The Scythians thus displaced the Cimmerians whose name occurs in the Crimean peninsula. They settled as nomads and semi-nomads in an area limited on the west by the Danube, on the east by the river Don. To the north the beginning of the woodland steppe may have set the boundary, although it is argued that Scythians penetrated as far as the region of Kiev. To the south lay the Mare Pontus, also called the Pontus Euxenios, the 'Welcoming Sea'; geographers of antiquity even compared the shape of the Black Sea to that of a Scythian bow.

What we know about the Scythians from antique sources are mostly reports written by their enemies; these are not very flattering and not altogether reliable. The Scythians were often ridiculed. They were fond of fermented camels' and horses' milk, called *kumys*, and therefore nicknamed 'milkeaters' (*galactophages*) and 'milkers of mares' (*hippemologes*). The Greek writer of comedies, Aristophanes, portrays them as great drunkards. In the 5th century BC when Greek towns and settlements on the southern boundaries of Scythia were flourishing, travellers' reports became more numerous. Olbia, the Greek colony near modern Odessa, a centre of trade, had its own northern caravan route, the northern Silk Road, to the East. The best account of the Scythians has come down to us from Herodotus of Halicarnassus, the 'Father of History'. In the middle of the 5th century BC Herodotus had himself journeyed to Olbia, and then further inland to Scythian territory. His accounts are now thought to be quite accurate, although much of his writings had been dismissed earlier on as being too far-fetched. In 9 AD during his exile to Tomi on the Romanian Black Sea coast, the poet Ovid wrote the *Tristia,* lamenting poems, and letters from exile, the *Epistulae ex Ponto.* In 95 AD a traveller from Asia Minor, the orator Dion Chrysostomos, described the town of Olbia in his *Borysthenitica.* But by then the town was already in decay and Scythian culture had vanished.

3 Scythian horseman with drawn bow

3   The Scythians emerge as fierce fighters and most accomplished riders. Horse and man seemed to create the perfect image of the 'centaur'. Horses were highly trained to respond to the rider's every wish and would kneel down to facilitate mounting, a life saving action to a heavily armed man. This flexibility in fighting, their great accuracy when using bow and arrows and their tactics of feigning withdrawal, only to lure the enemy into a trap, made the Scythian aggressors practically invincible. Herodotus says of them: 'A people without fortified towns, living, as the Scythians do, in waggons which they take with them wherever they go, accustomed, one and all, to fight on horseback with bows and arrows, and dependent for their food not upon agriculture but upon their cattle: how can such a people fail to defeat the attempt of an invader not only to subdue them, but even to make contact with them?' [14] The Scythians were also extremely fond of hunting, indeed fighting and hunting seemed of equal importance. Again Herodotus illustrates this point: having arrayed themselves in battle formation under their king Idanthyrsus and facing the Persian army of Darius with their cavalry and infantry, '... as soon as their dispositions were made, a hare started up between the two armies and began running. The Scythians were after it in a moment — company after company of them, directly they caught sight of it — while the army was reduced to a shouting rabble.'[15] Darius then withdrew his army, so deeply had his pride been hurt by the Scythian action.

Scythian weapons were plentiful: the battle-axe, long and short swords, daggers, clubs, ball and chain, pickaxes, javelins, lances, bows and highly poisonous arrows. A powerful whip, the *nagaika*, the whip of 'nine tails', was used for wolf hunting as well as in battle. No other people of antiquity have provided the archaeologists with grave finds of such a variety of weaponry. The Scythians were head hunters, a common thing amongst archaic people. The amount of skulls a man possessed passed for a proof of courage, and enemy scalps decorated the reins of the horses. It was also a sign of rank to tattoo the body. When out hunting or as advance guard at the beginning of a battle, bowmen might have ridden with bare chests, although the main army was well protected with shields and armour. The bowmen used their arrows with great accuracy and it is said that the many thousands of arrows sent off at a time obscured the sun.

4 Two Scythians with drinking horn

4   The Scythians concluded fraternal rites: two men would seal a pact of life by mixing their blood with wine '. . . then they dip into the bowl a sword, some arrows, a battle-axe, and a javelin, and speak a number of prayers; lastly, the two contracting parties and their chief followers drink the mixture of wine and blood,'[16] sharing the bowl or the drinking horn between two people. Such bonds entailed great faithfulness and readiness to sacrifice their own life for the sake of their blood-brother's. They could take on great hardships in defending their beliefs and their honour. Sympathizing with other cults or customs was not tolerated. We know of king Scylas, who had been attracted to the Greek cult of Dionysus during one of his frequent visits to the Greek settlement of Olbia, '. . . and no Scythian can see sense in imagining a god who drives people out of their wits . . . when the Scythians saw their king in the grip of the Bacchic frenzy, they were profoundly disturbed and, returning to the army, let every man know of the disgraceful spectacle they had witnessed.'[17] Scylas had to flee the country and was eventually beheaded by his half-brother, the new king. We also know of Anacharsis, 'a great traveller, and a man of great and varied knowledge', who offered sacrifice to a foreign mother goddess and was immediately shot dead by the king himself, who was also his brother.

The Scythians believed in life after death. A dead leader was joined in the tomb by members of his family and by his servants and his horses. A year after the death of a king a second ceremony took place: fifty of the best of the king's remaining servants were killed, their bodies propped up on their dead horses and arrayed outside the tomb to form a forbidding and ghostly funerary guard. The embalmed bodies of Scythian chiefs and their wives were buried with their favourite belongings: garments embroidered with small golden plaques, head ornaments, costly weapons, horses and precious horse-gear, wagons, silver, gold and bronze jewellery, household artefacts, cooking and lighting devices, such as bronze candelabras, cushions, carpets and tapestries, food and wine. Herodotus reported that after a burial the Scythians would burn hemp seeds on red-hot stones inside a small tent. He did not realize that they were in fact inhaling a powerful drug, *hauma* (*cannabis sativa*), possibly related to the Indian *soma*, and explained that the Scythians used this unsurpassed 'vapour bath' as a process to cleanse their bodies and that they 'enjoy it so much that they howl with pleasure.' [18]

The graves were chambers dug deep into the ground with connecting corridors, side chambers and access shafts. A great amount of earth and stones piled up on top of these graves formed the *kurgan* up to 20 m high. [19] The top layer of these mounds was made up from turf taken from fertile land and often brought over a considerable distance as an assurance that the dead chief would not be left without his pastures. It is thought that most *kurgans* had stone steles placed on their summits, images of stags or roughly carved figures of a warrior, the *kamennaja baba.*

5

5 Scythian *kamennaja baba*

As nomads the Scythians would travel to winter and summer pastures and transport their houses, felt yurts or 'basket' type of huts, on carts; thus whole towns seemed to be on the move. Children's clay toys have been found showing such cart houses of different shapes and sizes. Recent excavations have surprisingly brought to light the existence of fortifications in the area of the lower Dnieper, similar to the Celtic *oppida.* Trading along the north coast of the Black Sea eventually encouraged the Scythians to establish permanent settlements.

In the 18th century Czar Peter the Great of Russia became aware of bronze and gold objects of great antiquity found in the Ukraine and in Siberia. Their exact provenance was often unknown. They were mostly finds from robbed graves and had so far escaped being melted down. We have to thank the taste and foresight of the Russian ruler who created the first collection of Scythian art. Since then archaeologists have more or less systematically explored the *kurgans,* often to find that they had been robbed in past years. The museums of St. Petersburg, Moscow and Kiev now house these precious objects which are but a few remaining from once huge hoards of grave goods.

In art the Scythian 'wild animal style' flourished from the end of the 7th to the 4th century BC, and to understand the zoomorphic images, realistic and fantastic creatures, we have to go back to the Eurasian steppe lands as the nomads had once experienced them. Since then the Ukraine steppe lands, the home grounds of the western Scythians, have been turned into highly productive granaries, the famous falls of the river Dnieper have been changed and the most spectacular of them covered by a reservoir. The lower course of the river once divided its flow into many smaller streams creating hundreds of islands with reeds and rushes, willows and woods, where birds were plentiful and wild boar, stags and elks used to roam. A traveller of the 19th century [20] describes the old vegetation of the steppes as an interminable sea of high grasses, but also comprising large stretches covered with herbs such as cumin, vermouth, lavender and sage. Sweet peas, tulips, irises, hyacinths, crocuses, melilots, mignonettes, spurges and Aaron's rod would spread over large areas. The same traveller stated very pointedly that the law of the grasslands was movement: movement of winds, movement of cattle and nomads, movement of swift horses. Nor was the steppe silent. A multitude of sounds rose from the land: the rustling of grasses touched by the wind, the humming of insects, the cry of birds and wild animals, the dull thundering of moving cattle and the shrieking and neighing of wild stallions rising against each other, their hooves clashing together like shields meeting in battle — a heraldic image which survived in Asian and Celtic art for many hundreds of years.

6 Panther in rolled animal style

7 Elk on a bird's claw

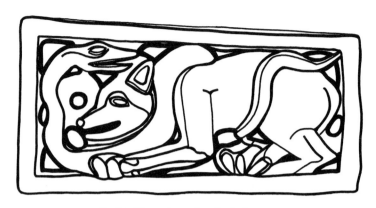

8 Wolf and snake fighting

Seen against this background we begin to understand the careful observation of animal life in Scythian bronzes: stone martens and small bears stretching out and in a playful mood intertwining themselves into graceful figures, wild cats rolling themselves up into circles, birds of prey swooping down on to unsuspecting victims and coils of clustered snakes moving on the ground. The wheel of life and death was for ever turning. It was not surprising that fantastic animals, half lion or bull, half eagle, winged horses and griffins would be added to the already rich repertoire of nature; virtues and characteristics of real animals were thus singled out and highlighted in art, and their magical and protective properties transmitted to the people.

6, 7, 8

9, 10

9 Two fabulous beasts from procession,
on golden scabbard

Diodorus Siculus, a Greek historian of the 1st century BC, related in what high esteem wild animals were held. The Scythian philosopher Anacharsis was asked by King Croesus of Lydia, who amongst all living beings was the most courageous, the most just and the wisest. Croesus had expected Anacharsis to name him as the protagonist of all these virtues but the philosopher answered: the wild animals were the most courageous beings, for they alone would die readily for their freedom; the wild animals also were the most just of all beings, for they lived according to nature and not according to laws, and nature was the work of the gods but laws only the work of men. And therefore the wild animals were also the wisest, for they held the truth of nature in higher esteem than the laws of men. Croesus was very disappointed with this answer and laughed it off as being tinged by the primitive life-style of a Scythian.[21]

10 Fabulous beast, on horse bridle

The Scythians were well acquainted with the high Caucasian mountain passes and made good use of the central Daryal Pass, the 'Scythian Way' to the south, during their warfare in the Near East. Herodotus tells a vivid tale about battles and skirmishes and pacts undertaken by Scythian rulers, but this summing up by the 'father of history' probably condenses the events of some hundred years into the saga of one big war. Metallurgy, ceramic styles and fort building had already established a cultural link in the Pontic-Anatolian areas during early Indo-European times. By the 7th century BC the Scythians established themselves in parts of north and south-west Iran and metallurgical skills from Iranian bronze and iron working centres began to make an impact on the Scythian way of life. Iranian towns such as Hassanlu, Ziwiyeh and Marlik, situated in the area between lake Urmia and the Caspian Sea, and the realm of Urartu in the highlands around lake Van, had developed a very original style which greatly influenced Scythian

11, 12
41, 42, 43

nomadic art. The style of Urartu in particular predominated over all other centres. Early Urartian art had relied on Assyrian, Syrian and Hittite–Aramaean sources. [22] Tulip-shaped designs, already known from Assur and Babylon, were shown on the haunches of bulls and lions; the turning sun–rosette and a pattern resembling a large M or W shaped sign decorated the bodies of lions and of stags. In addition lines would terminate in scroll-like squiggles or circles, so that the style came to be known as the 'ringlet-style'. Certain Scythian motifs, such as a new emphasis on animals arranged in pairs and the combination of hetero-

13

geneous animals — the bird-lion and bull creatures with inter-changing zoomorphic elements — were inspired by Urartu and the style of Luristan in south-west Iran. Scythian art is the outcome of the assimilation of Iranian culture into nomadic traditions.

11 Lion. Urartian

12 Winged lion. Ziwiyeh

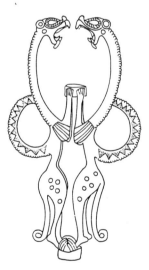

13 Twin elongated beasts. Luristan

Chapter 4

The Eastern Scythians

Antiquity mentions 'two Scythian lands', thus including large tribes of Asian Scythians. Persians and Indians called the Asiatic Scythians the *saka*. They occupied the vast grasslands stretching out to the east: from the Volga and the Ural Mountains over Kazakhstan to the Altai Mountains and the Mongolian Plateau. These areas were also settled by other ethnic tribes, but the Scythians were the dominating force. East of the Caspian Sea lived the *saka haumavarga* — 'the hauma drinkers' — and the *saka tigraxanda* — the 'saka of the pointed hats'.[23]

By the second millennium BC Indo-Iranian steppe tribes had penetrated into southern Siberia and Central Asia and established a cultural unity of Asian nomad tribes. Siberia and Mongolia were lived in by Europoid and Mongoloid tribes and only towards the end of the first millennium BC did Mongolian characteristics take over. A constant intermingling of Caucasian Europoid and Mongoloid races in Siberian areas resulted in the use of different languages and their many regional variants. But despite regional variations the art of the steppe was not based on ethnic differences but showed a remarkable uniformity, partly due to the developing knowledge of metal working which created a cultural exchange over a vast area. 'All that we learn of cultural movement in inner Asia and central Asia, both in the Early Bronze Age and in the later period of full steppe nomadism, predisposes us to accept the fact of almost incredibly rapid transmission of types of metal artefacts over great distances.'[24]

Trade thus linked vast areas over vast distances and the Scythian style travelled from the Mare Pontus to the river Yenisey and Lake Baikal in southern Siberia, and well beyond to China and Korea. We are thus faced with a great cultural continuum over a long period. The Indo–Iranian traditions of the steppe tribes were constantly nourished by influences from Persia (todays Iran) and Mesopotamia. Assyrian and Sumerian art of an earlier date was still alive. But if the images of Iranian griffins, tigers and zoomorphic creatures infiltrated China, Chinese bronzes at some period also travelled west and in turn influenced inner Asian styles. The 'mysterious cousinship' between the Shang (ca 16th – 11th century BC) and Asian tribes has always had its fascination. [25]

Valuable information about Scythian art, trade and life style has reached us from the Pazyryk area of the Altai, where the burial chambers of the *kurgans* had filled with water, which subsequently turned into ice and thus preserved the contents. Amongst the finds were cowry shells from the Indian Ocean, coriander seeds from Central Asia and the Near East, gold and silver objects and woollen cloths from Iran, and the oldest known wool carpet, also from Iran or Turkmenistan, silks and mirrors from China, and a Scythian harp. Felt appliqué work and work in wood, leather, bone, horn and wool show animal motifs of the steppe, the wolf, the elk, the ibex (*capra sibirica*) and different species of birds. Gold and bronze objects take up the same theme and images of the lion, the ram and the fish are combined with fantastic animal variations, such as those of the griffin with cat–like ears, a mane and a cock's crest. Warriors found in the Pazyryk graves may also be described as *Picti* ; their bodies were covered with tattoo markings, a sign of nobility. Far away in Tadjik burials of the Oxus district, clay death masks with tattoo designs forward proof of similar customs. The horses found in rich graves which had joined their masters in death were not of the local steppe breed but of refined Central Asian stock.

14

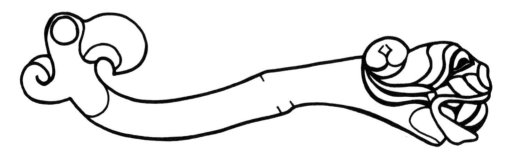

14 Snaffle with animal and bird heads. Pazyryk

Pockets of steppe culture have also been found in the highland region of Tuva in the northern Altai and in the southern Siberian area of todays Minusinsk by the river Yenisey. The people of the upper Yenisey belonged to the Tagar culture. Sheltered by mountains and woodlands they remained semi-nomadic and formed the last outpost of Eurasian Europoid tribes. Their metal artefacts and even weapons were executed in bronze and not in iron, as was the case in the more advanced western districts. The 'wild animal style' of their bronzes is rounded and realistic; fantastic creatures seem to be lacking, but scenes of animal fights and heraldic motifs still uphold the Scythian traditions of the steppe. Tagar weapons and Tagar art reached eastern Europe but also Korea, North China (Ordos bronzes) and Mongolia.

15

15 Bronze mirror disc with two entwined animals. Tuva

The Tagar people placed orthostats engraved with human masks or figures taken over from earlier civilizations, on their burial grounds. Tagar rock pictures with stag images seen on the stones of the river Yenisey and Tagar shamanistic stories and myths form a valuable contribution to the appreciation of Scytho-Sakian beliefs. [26]

Chapter 5

Animal Magic and Shamanism

With the exception of the small cult figure of the stone warrior placed on the summit of the western *kurgans* and some engraved steles positioned around the flat stone graves of the Karasuk culture of the Baikal areas,[27] and before Greek influence prevailed, Scythians did not portray their gods or heroes. We know from Herodotus that they honoured the gods of the sky, the sun and the earth, but we have to go to the religions of India, Persia and Mesopotamia in order to appreciate these beliefs which were fundamental to Indo-Iranian, even pre-Vedic, times.

From Scythian myths, such as are still told in our days by the Osset people of the Terek area of the Caucasus, we learn about heroes belonging to the world of gods and we are told what limits such a world created for men. But both Irish and Osset sagas have in common that gods and heroes cannot be clearly defined or differentiated, since they merge into one personality. Scythian gods come to us more directly, but still mysteriously, through the magic of the animal world, so profusely illustrated in Scytho-Siberian art. But even then the picture is not clear, for we approach a world of spells which does not lend itself to be easily deciphered. We have to content ourselves with the knowledge that it was common for tribes to adopt an animal as their symbol and that the many zoomorphic images had once represented a sort of talisman. Archaic beliefs in a kinship between man and the animal world were of great importance in Scytho-Siberian traditions. Animals personified the forces of creation and destruction and formed part of obscure rites already discernible in the early mysteries of Palaeolithic times.

Scythian bronzes and superbly executed work in gold and silver charm by their stylistic variations and great liveliness within a given form, such as that represented by the 'rolled animal style', *16* and by images of animals opposing each other or engaged in fight, and by the stag turned back on itself. The real 'charms', however, are the hidden elements of underlying magic. Animals represented universal qualities to which man himself aspired and which he tried to maintain in order to survive: prowess in battle and expertise in the interpretation of sounds while out hunting or fighting, swiftness and agility, and an obstinate determination to succeed.

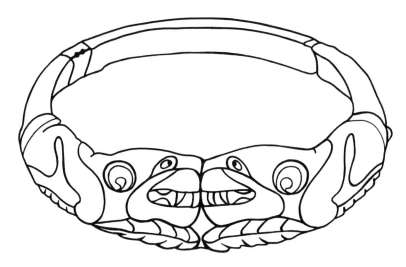

16 Bronze torque with tigers, from Siberia

17   The stag was one of the animals most often represented, in Scythian as well as in Pictish art. It is thought that the root of the word *saka* is related to 'stag' and that in fact the Scythians may have called themselves the 'stag people'. In Siberian art the stag or elk could be shown as representing the whole universe — its back was outlined as a mountain range, its fur represented the woodlands, even the flies on its back were compared to birds; it rested on eight legs and any change in this position caused underground tremors.

The stag is primarily not an aggressive animal. It therefore comes as a surprise that it should serve as emblem to a war-like people. But the stag is hunted and life is as precarious for him as it is for the tribe. A carrier of cosmic forces — his antlers act as sensitive antennae to earth rays — he also embodies the hero whose strength derives from the sun. Siberian myths tell us that the stag or elk travels along the sky during the day as a gigantic sun-like image. The nomads knew him as the 'elk-sun' and portrayed him as a golden being carrying the sun on his antlers. The identification with the sky and the cosmos also takes place during the night. Like the stars which continually displace each other on their nightly

45

trail, the stag races across the night sky for he is being hunted by a mysterious hunter, Aroma-Tellje, the god of thunder, who follows the stag with bow and fiery arrows. Not yet, say the old Siberian stories, has Aroma-Tellje succeeded in hitting the stag. But he will eventually do so and the third arrow to enter the stag's body will also portend the end of the world. Some tribes see Aroma-Tellje as a mighty bear, a hunter who never rests during the night.

17 Stag, wood with leather antlers and ears. From Pazyryk, Altai

The stag symbolizes life and death. Tungusian rock pictures show the stag swimming across the waters of the river of the dead. The rocks of the Yenisey area depict boats transporting people who wear antlers as head ornaments. Such symbolism has become remote to us, but we can occasionally still trace the original source of such stories. A.P. Okladnikov relates the experience of a young Siberian nomad of our times who saw a stag crossing a river while the setting sun seemed to sink into the same golden waters and that, during the intensity of this moment of beholding, the old myths of his people seemed to reach out to him in their full impact. [28]
18 The stele of a stag which used to stand on the summit of a chief warrior's grave symbolized the rising sun and therefore the

promise of a new life.

The stag is also closely related to the mirror, the reflecting disc which symbolized the sun's circle, and fire. Indo-Iranian societies have always linked three fires: the fire of the sun, the fire of the sky (as lightning), and the fires on earth, such as the hearth fire and the sacrificial fire. Fire was also associated with the forging of weapons and with war. The gong of war and the shiny metal disc of the mirror can both represent the same cosmic force. The Pictish mirror is thus not primarily a lady's accessory, and we will later see that, although it is indeed used by a lady, she is the Indo-Iranian goddess of war, and the sister or wife of the sun god.

18 Stag-stone. Baikal region. Karasuk culture

A man who stood in direct communication with the spirits of animals and of the world beyond was the shaman. Clad in animal skins and hung with charms, he acted as the mediator between the world of the dead and the world of the living. He was a healer, a rescuer of souls, a soothsayer. A woman who performed the same tasks was a shamaness. Very seldom did the shaman choose his vocation. It was a difficult one involving initiation, deprivation and to a certain extent asceticism. False predictions were severely punished by the community. A shaman was not so much elected by his people, but he was singled out by spirits, often but not always at an early time of his life. A refusal to follow his spiritual calling would lose him his inner balance and result in illness and madness. The shaman was a seer and a sorcerer, he possessed mastery over fire, water and air. He had his breath from the wind and his eyes from the sun.

To the shaman animals were guides of the soul. They were closely connected with the 'other world' of the ancestors; during initiation rites their characteristics and virtues were taken up by the shaman who chose one or several animals as his helpers. The shaman trained himself to understand the language of animals and during his ecstasy all ordinary limits were transcended for he

19

20

would be able to speak with their voices. Animals thus provided a source of strength and became totem images. Aquatic birds, the snake and the fish related to the Underworld, where the Great Mother of all Beings lived. When the shaman crossed the river of death in a boat fish swam at the prow and showed him the way. The myths of the ocean of the dead also explain the mysterious link between fish and horse. The horse enabled the shaman to fly into the heavens or to travel into the Underworld; it was capable of breaking through spiritual planes of existence and pass over into other worlds. In this capacity the horse was a funerary animal and we begin to understand the many horse sacrifices in Scythian burials. As a mythical image of death the horse formed part of a shaman's ecstatic experience. In Indo-Iranian mythology the horse was linked to the god of war and thunder and atmosphere, the god who links sun and earth.

19 Duck and fish on symbol stone from **Easterton of Roseisle**

20 Twin horses with fish tails on cross-slab in **Aberlemno** churchyard

To the shaman our world existed on three levels: those of the heavens, of the earth and of the Underworld. The link between these different planes of existence was the *axis mundi*, the pole or Tree of Life, which stretched from the centre of the earth to the highest heavens. Persian, Islamic and Christian mythologies speak of a bridge to astral zones. The rainbow, the ladder, the rope and the spiral could all fulfil the same purpose; the central opening through which these mystical steps passed was also called the navel. Scythian elaborately wrought silver and gilt *omphalos* (navel) plates were the property of chiefs and could also be carried as small replicas as lucky tokens attached to the belt. A disc with a circle in the middle was a symbol of the earth's open door, the centre symbolizing a sacred space, and when in trance, the shaman or his assistant would step through such a doorway into another world. They had to beware not to touch the sides of the inner circle, for the door was quick to close again thus barring the way of return. The spiritual journey implied a getting out of human time; the quickness of action needed in order to avoid the closing of the door of perception may be equated to a flash of lightning or the instantaneous enlightenment of religious inspiration. [29]

For every nomadic family the central pillar of the world was symbolized by their tent pole and the circular opening in the middle of their tent through which the hearth smoke escaped was also a door to heaven. The polar star represented another opening to the luminous universe beyond. A mountain could also be the central axis around which the world was turning. Indian myths mention the mysterious Mount Meru in this connection, and Babylonian temples and their ziggurat towers formed a parallel in architecture to the holy mountains of the Indo-Iranian world. The 'Tree of Life', the 'Cosmic Tree', which touched heaven with its top-most branches, was essential to shamanic ideology. A snake lived among its roots, for a snake had access to the Underworld; the bird of the sun, the eagle, perched on its top. Other birds, the spirits of unborn children, sat on its branches. The shaman's tent had a replica of such a tree, cut and trimmed of its bark, placed by the entrance or under the central opening.

Aquatic birds were particularly venerated since they travelled freely between three worlds and could live on earth, in the water, and in the sky. A balanced straight flight, such as practised by the wild geese and ducks, was believed to have meditative qualities. Indeed, the more we learn about shamanic beliefs the more we realize that the magicians of the Tibetan Bon traditions, the Indian yogins and the Buddhist siddhas all built on the same 'primitive' religious experience, the 'millennial metaphysical speculation of

India', as M. Eliade calls it.[30]

The shaman's task was that of combatting demons, disease and forces of black magic. He provided defence and protection for the living and guidance for the souls of the dead during their journey to the Nether regions. Only by going through an ecstatic experience and by travelling the supernatural worlds could the shaman achieve his aim, to recover a 'primordial human condition', akin to a paradisal situation. [31] His ecstatic flights to the sun and the moon, his journeys to the centre of the earth, were always accompanied by the primeval sound of the drum, which played a major part in the shaman's magico-religious interpretation of the complex forces ruling the world. The tree from which the wood of the drum was taken became the shaman's own 'Tree of Life', and the animal skin from which the drum was made became a means to metamorphosis, since it determined the ancestor whose spirit acted as a vital help to the shaman when transcending human condition. Stringed instruments, dance and incantations also introduced trance, but the most powerful sound to attract benevolent spirits was still that of the drum, sometimes called the 'singing bow'.

One of the most characteristic archaic symbols of death, maladies and seemingly unsolvable problems was the knot. It impeded the flow of life and was therefore frequently related to the world of demons. But an elaborately tied knot could also be placed in the way of destructive influences and in such a case it became a talisman and active force to ensure good fortune.

As an attribute of his status the shaman carried with him a sling: a demoniacal device which could become a snare, a noose, even a net or a chain. In the hands of the shaman, however, the sling had a positive connotation, ensuring healing and deliverance, for with its help the shaman would retrieve a soul lost in the Underworld and guide it back to its owner whose health would then be restored, just as the soul of a dying creature — man or sacrificial animal — could be caught in the sling and taken to its protective deities. But even more ambitiously the shaman used the sling to catch the sky and bind sun and earth. Under the sanskrit name of *pásha* the sling played an important part in Indian Tantric and later Buddhist mythology, as indeed did many basic shamanistic speculations which lend themselves to be developed into most complex philosophies. 'Gods who Bind', and whose representative the shaman could be, were basic to archaic religious thinking and

21

the linking of sun and earth through the god of wind and atmosphere formed part of ancient Indo-Iranian, even pre-Vedic, beliefs. In the steppe regions of Minusinsk incised rock pictures of the second millennium BC show such a linking of discs or astral bodies, and we shall see in a later chapter how the Picts traced the same motif on their stones and defined it very clearly.

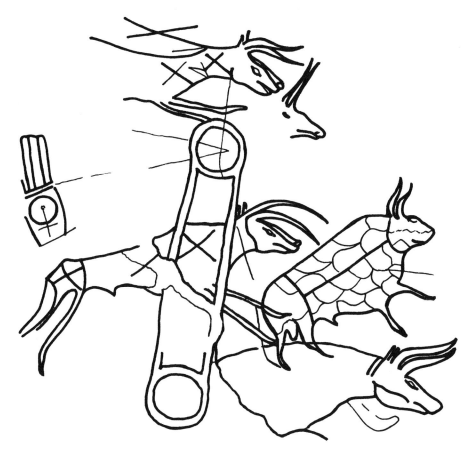

21 Rock drawings, Minusinsk steppe region

Chapter 6

The Ossetes and the Great Goddess

In the Terek area of the Caucasus live a folk of north Iranian origin, the Ossetes. [32] They are the direct descendants of the Alans, Sarmatian tribes belonging to the Sauromatians. According to Herodotus the *Sauromatae* took their origin from the union of Scythian warriors and the legendary Amazons. [33]

The old Ossetian language is related to the Scythian language, and as living protagonists of ancient traditions these people have been studied by historians and linguists since the 18th century. The stories of their forefathers, the mythical Nart, are the only surviving Scythian legends so far. A very strong Scythian character emerges which centres on prowess in battle, linked to a heroism with complete disregard for danger and deprivations. Like the Picts the Ossetes may have adhered to matrilinear succession. [34]

The legends tell us that their kind derived from a mysterious being, a woman who lived under the sea but could also turn herself into a bird. Her father was the mighty Donbettir, ruler of waters. A liaison with her established the beginning of new generations, but as two brothers had to die fighting each other on her behalf, the uncertainty of human fate and its implications are already indicated. [35] The daughter of the sea woman, born out of the dead mother's grave, became the central character in the stories of the Nart, for ever holding all mysterious threads of destiny in her hands. The links to the sea and the rivers remain strong.

22

22 The Great Goddess
with wings and volute limbs.
Greco-Scythian

One of the favourite subjects of Scythian art is the frontal image of a winged woman with snake legs. The image of the snake goes far back in history and possibly belongs to a non-Aryan substratum with ancient Tantric leanings. The snake can rise from the waters to the surface of the earth, and 'her' efficiency was used in rain rites. By emerging from the depths of the earth and by providing beneficient rain to the land the snake symbolizes 'life', but her deadly poison also makes her into a messenger of the Under-world. Thus the snake moves freely between two worlds, and like a goddess who represents the characteristics of the god whom she accompanies, she can evolve male or female qualities. Herodotus relates that according to mythical sources the Scythian people came out of the union of Herakles with a snake woman who lived in the woodlands of Hylaia; he also mentions a second version which states that the first man was Targitaos, a son of Zeus and of a daughter of the river Borysthenes.[36] The Ossetes describe the goddess as 'damp, strong and without fault'. She illustrates the archaic knowledge that men and animals are indebted to the same life force which can create or destroy. The Nartian snake woman as the mother of man-

23

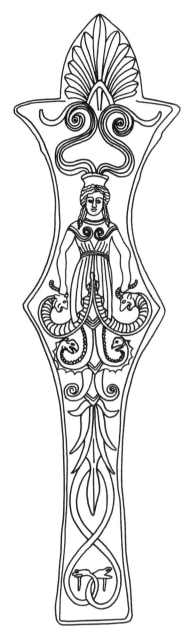

23 The Great Goddess with snake limbs

kind implies this duality. Hinduism [37] transmits us a very clear picture of her seemingly contradictory potentials: the Indian goddess Maha-Lakshmi, the Great Lakshmi, is the symbol of fertility, beauty and happiness; another aspect of her nature, the goddess Durga, implies destruction; as Kali, an emanation of Durga, the goddess becomes the personification of time as well as of its final dissolution.[38]

Siberian myths relate that a giant snake helped to trace out the world. Hinduism gives a different orientation to this shamanistic picture: magical elements are transported into a god-made world, for we learn that Vishnu, supreme god of creation and continuation, rests on a giant snake which floats on the waters of the Cosmic Ocean before he wakes from a deep contemplative sleep to create a new world-cycle. Vishnu is related to solar energy as the offspring of the sun and the great Vedic Earth Mother, Aditi. Vishnu's consort, Lakshmi, takes over from Aditi in later cults and becomes the Great Goddess with friendly and destructive qualities.

24

25

26

Lakshmi is seen in the symbolic sign of happiness, the Indian *shrivatsa* sign. In its more abstracted version this sign combines lotuses, fish and snake tails. As Lakshmi's attributes were associated with the element 'water' Indian art also shows her divine image, or her symbols, being attended by elephants spurting water out of their trunks and bathing the goddess.

24 *Shrivatsa,* sign of happiness

25 *Shrivatsa* as symbol of fertility

26 *Shrivatsa* symbol being bathed by elephants

A silver bowl found at Gundestrup (Denmark) and probably dating from the first half of the first century BC, shows Celtic elements in its design while some of the iconographical motifs have their equivalents in Thracian silver work. Flemming Kaul argues persuasively that the style of the cauldron derived from the Celtic Scordisci tribe who in the 3rd century BC had partly settled in Thracian country.[39] One of the inside panels depicts the Great *27* Goddess surrounded by the animals which represent her different aspects. The elephants on the upper half of the panel emphasize her Indian character as goddess of beauty and fertility, while her martial presence is asserted by the sun-rosettes and the lion, symbols of her Mesopotamian counterpart, the goddess Ishtar. The precise associations of the griffins are unknown, but they are possibly a symbol of destruction.

27 The Great Goddess on the Gundestrup cauldron

Earlier Celtic art of Hallstatt and La Tène may have hinted at the appearance of the goddess in anthropoid designs, but her actual picture was lost, like so many other straightforward images in Celtic abstracted ornamental designs. We can, however, still trace the Scythian combination of *28* woman and snake and the Indian *shrivatsa* symbol in Celtic metal work, such as seen on *29* the helmet from Canosa di Puglia (Bari), from the first half of the 4th century BC, and on a *30* bronze fitting in the form of a horse's head from Stanwick (Yorkshire) from the 1st century BC.

28 Indian fish symbol of happiness

29 Crest of the Great Goddess on Celtic helmet

The 'crest' of the Great Goddess may also be detected on Pictish stones in the form of similar spiral patterns. It is seen on the lower part of the *31* damaged symbol stone of **Abernethy**, on the Pl. 7 **Hilton of Cadboll** stone, and on a lead disc from *32* the **Brough of Birsay**, as well as other background panels such as **Shandwick**. Twin spiral symbols were known in Hittite Anatolia, *33* and in ancient Mesopotamia they were symbols of the Great Mother as a fertility goddess, and hung as ornaments from necklaces.

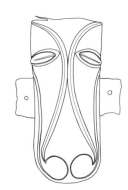

30 Crest of the Great Goddess on Celtic bronze fitting in the form of a horse's head

31 Symbol stone at **Abernethy**

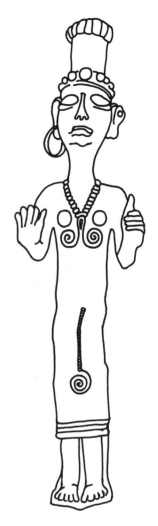

32 Lead disc from **Brough of Birsay**

33 Spiral breast-ornament on Syrian bronze figurine

The Mesopotamian *omega* symbol [40] (below), commonly found on Babylonian *kudurru* (boundary) stones, is associated with mother goddesses and possibly with Ishtar herself. Replicas of such a symbol appear above the cross on the front of the **Maiden Stone**, Chapel of Garioch, on the **Brodie Stone** and at the top of the symbol stone at **Aberlemno** roadside, where they assume the graceful shapes of opposing beasts or a snake.

piece 8

NOTES TO PART I

1   J.P. Mallory, *In Seach of the Indo-Europeans*, p. 195: 'The Eneolithic is generally marked by the addition of copper artefacts to the otherwise Neolithic stone technology.'

2   The Andronovo people of Kazakhstan and Uzbekistan are often termed early Indo-Europeans. Their territories were the homelands of later Iron Age Eastern Iranians — the Saka, Massagetae, Sarmatians and Alans.

3   Nora Chadwick, *The Celts*, London, 1971, pp. 36,38. Venceslas Kruta, 'In Search of Ancient Celts', in *The Celts*, Exhibition catalogue, Venice, 1991, p. 30

4   J.P. Mallory, *op. cit.*, p. 71: 'The current state of our knowledge of Greek dialects can accommodate Indo-Europeans entering Greece at any time between 2200 and 1600 BC to emerge later as Greek speakers.'

5   Julius Caesar, *De Bello Gallico.*

6   Georges Dumézil, *L'idéologie tripartie des Indo-Européens*, pp. 20–27, 58–61. Comprehensive and carefully researched interpretations of Celtic myths are to be found in the *Lexikon der Keltischen Mythologie*, by Sylvia and Paul F. Botheroyd, Diederichs Verlag, Munich, 1992.

7   Bede, *Ecclesiastical History of the English People*, translated by Leo Sherley-Price, revised by R.E.Latham, Book I,1

8   J.Gantz, *Early Irish Myths and Sagas*, London, 1981, p. 246

9   *Ibid*, p. 252

10 *Ibid*, p. 125

11 G. S. Mac Eoin, 'On the Irish Legend of the Origin of the Picts', *Studia Hibernica* No. 4, Dublin, 1964, pp. 138–154

12 K. H. Jackson, 'The Pictish Language', in *The Problem of the Picts*, 1955, p. 159

13 Fatma Turkkan-Wille, 'Nomaden und Könige— Die Skythen', in *Aus den Schatzkammern Eurasiens*, Kunsthaus Zürich, 1993, p. 46

14 Herodotus,*The Histories*, Book IV, 46. (Transl. A. de Selincourt, revised A.R. Burn, London, 1972).

15 *Ibid*, IV, 131

16 *Ibid*, IV, 71

17 *Ibid*, IV, 80

18 *Ibid,* IV, 76

19 *Kurgan* is the Russian name for the barrow or hill-grave found particularly in eastern Europe and western Siberia. The practice of *kurgan* burial has been traced back to cultures occupying the steppe and forest-steppe of the southern areas of Ukraine and Russia by the 4th millennium BC, possibly originating in the Volga-Ural region. The renowned archaeologist Marija Gimbutas has argued that the

kurgan people are the Proto-Indo-Europeans, and this is accepted by many archaeologists and linguists. The Scythian *kurgans*, unique in their number, size and the richness of their grave goods, and often called the 'pyramids of the steppes', were complex and labour-consuming constructions, containing enormous catacombs in the case of 'royal' *kurgans*.

20 J. G. Kohl, *Reisen in Südrussland*, 1841, mentioned by R. Rolle, *Die Welt der Skythen*, Frankfurt, 1980, pp. 17–18

21 R. Rolle, *ibid*, p. 145

22 André Parrot places the beginnings of an Urartian bronze style as early as the 9th century BC.

23 R. Rolle, *op. cit.*, p. 47

24 W. Watson, *Cultural Frontiers in Ancient East Asia*, Edinburgh, 1971, p. 54

25 W. Watson, *ibid*, p. 50. It is not clear when exactly the Chinese Bronze Age started. The most general view suggests the 16th century BC and there is some doubt whether it was an indigenous development or a cultural borrowing from Mesopotamia, where the Bronze Age had already started by the third millennium BC.

26 As early as the fourth millennium BC an expansion of Indo-European people from the Pontic-Caspian homelands into Asia resulted in what we now call the Afanasievo culture, situated as far east as the Minusinsk basin and the Altai regions, and possibly reaching south into Chinese Turkestan. Their successors were the genetically unrelated people of the Okunevo culture.

Towards the middle of the second millennium BC, if not earlier, the Indo-Iranian Andronovo culture of Europoid types of people began to be established in the area between the Urals and the river Yenisey. The Andronovo culture is thought today to have consisted of many regional variants of independent traditions. It stretched from the northern border of the forest steppe as far south as the Pamirs of Tadzhikistan. From about 1300–800 BC the Mongoloid Karasuk culture continued the Andronovo traditions in southern Siberia and central Kazakhstan, including the area of the lower Syr Darya and areas in the Tien Shan mountains. During the following centuries the Karasuk culture continued to survive as a late Bronze Age culture in the steppe lands around Minusinsk, an area sheltered from outside influences by high mountains and dense woodland.

Traditions of the Karasuk culture survived in the following Europoid Tagar culture of Minusinsk, which lasted to the first century BC. Around 700 BC many tribes had become fully nomadic, but the Tagar people continued to lead a semi-nomadic life with summer and winter pastures.

The highland region of Tuva, south of Minusinsk, created its own
nomadic style during the 7th -2nd centuries BC.
All these centres, of the Altai, the Yenisey, and of Tuva maintained
strong Scytho-Sakian links despite their regional differentiations.
Their art was not based on ethnic Mongoloid or Europoid differences
but on a way of life which all the steppe people had in common.

27   Some stone figures used on Karasuk and Tagar graves may date from
the earlier Tasmin civilization of about 3000 BC.

28   The Siberian stories of the stag and the elk have been taken from A. P.
Okladnikov, *Der Hirsch mit dem Goldenen Geweih* , Wiesbaden, 1972.

29   W. von Rubruk, *Reisen zum Grosskhan der Mongolen* , 1253-55,
Stuttgart, 1984, p. 145, mentions in his descriptions of the Mongolian
habits of the thirteenth century AD that, when entering the tent of the
Khan, it was forbidden, on pain of death, to touch the threshhold of the
doorway of the ruler's yurt.

30   M. Eliade, *Shamanism* , London, 1964, p. 405

31   M. Eliade, *ibid* , p. 171

32   The Iranians of the pre-Christian era should not be confused with today's
Persian state of Iran. The original meaning of Iranian goes back to
Aryanam , the 'land of the Arya', pre-Vedic tribes who invaded India at
the beginning of the second millennium BC and spread from north-west
India and the Punjab to the Euphrates and to Syria.

33   Herodotus, *op. cit.* , IV, 105 ff.

34   Bede, *op. cit.* , Book I, 1

35   Legends involving twin brothers and godly companions who are doomed
recur frequently in the nomadic world. Myths tend to see in twins
representatives of natural elements in opposition which cannot be
reconciled. The biblical twins Cain and Abel, and the mythical founders
of Rome, Romulus and Remus, are condemned by fate to fail in their joint
ventures. 'Happier' twins with complementary characteristics are the
Roman Dioscuri, Castor and Pollux, and the Indian Ashvin brothers.

36   Herodotus, *op. cit.* , IV, 8-10, and IV, 5-7

37   The oldest known Indian culture, that of Dravidian speaking people,
was found through excavations in the Indus Valley at two main sites,
Harappa and Mohenjo-daro. It may date from about 2500 BC. Towards
2000 BC Aryan tribes invaded north-west India. The Dravidians were
driven further south and the Indus culture was replaced by the Aryan-
Vedic epoch which lasted from about 1600-800 BC. The Aryans
introduced religious teachings, the Vedas; the oldest parts of the Vedas
date from before the first millennium BC, but were only written down

as mythic-religious texts, crystallised into the philosophies of the
Vedanta , at the beginning of our era. The great Indian epic poems,
the *Ramayana* and the *Mahabharata* , the 18 *Puranas* and other religious
writings partly date from a late Vedic period. They were evolved over
several hundred years and also included pre-Vedic thoughts. Through
Brahmanism, the cult of one god, Brahma, Vedic polytheism gave way
to a monotheistic philosophy. Buddhism and Jainism brought reforms —
Buddha lived from about 563-483 BC. The roots of early Buddhism cannot
be found in the soil of Vedic-Brahmanic tradition, but in a very ancient
Indian tradition, probably Dravidian, which also influenced the late Vedic
writings of the *Upanishads* . In order to survive, Brahmanism created
a kind of counter-reform. This new religious system developed into
Hinduism which became particularly strong in the first centuries of our
times, and again from the 6th century AD onwards. Hinduism as we
know it today integrated conceptions of Jainism and Buddhism and
is a relatively late development of Indian religion.

38   The female nature comprising both aspects of the goddess is expounded
in the Indian Shakta teachings.

39   'We shall probably never learn how the cauldron found its way to
Denmark. Perhaps it was brought back by Cimbri who on their raid
through Europe also had contacts with the Scordisci. The region of
Jutland where the cauldron is found still bears the name of the Cimbri
tribe — Himmerland.' Quotation from Flemming Kaul, 'The Gundestrup
Cauldron', in *The Celts,* Venice, *op. cit.* , p. 538

40   See also Part V, Chapter I, p. 189

* * *

PART II

Gods and Heroes

Chapter 1

The Sarcophagus of St. Andrews

Towards the end of the 6th century BC when the Scythians had driven the Persian army under Darius back over the Hellespont (513-12 BC) and when political pacts with Greece became desirable, Scythian art begins to undergo some changes. The influence of the Assyrian style of Urartu is slowly retreating and we find a strong appreciation of Greek elements. The predominance of a Greek style increases during the 4th century BC. Growing trade between Scythia and the Greek towns on the Black Sea, particularly in the area of the Bosphorus, encourages Greek taste. The image of man enters the Scythian world and narrative scenes become more frequent.

Pl. 1   The most striking example in the Pictish world of this realistic style is also the most treasured of all the Pictish stones in our possession: the front panel of the **Sarcophagus of St. Andrews**. Most of the pieces which now constitute the sarcophagus were found in 1833. They had probably been built into a sarcophagus in the 8th or 9th century AD and later been discarded and dug into the ground about six feet deep in the vicinity of St. Rule's Tower, by St. Andrews Cathedral. After the discovery of the slabs a sarcophagus was re-constructed in the style of Christian church furniture and the panels were dated to the 8th - 9th centuries AD.

Pl. 2   The panels which now form the sarcophagus are a narrative front panel framed by two decorative panels, and two side panels, one very fragmentary.

A very first look at the sarcophagus already reveals a great stylistic discrepancy between the narrative front panel and the side and end panels. It is indeed not difficult to recognize the 8th-9th century style of the christianized Pictish world in all the four smaller panels. The winding scrolls of the side panels, a combination of plant and animal life, are very similar to the sculptured design of the 'inhabited vine scroll' in Northumbrian style on the Anglo-Saxon Ruthwell Cross, Dumfriesshire, on the Bewcastle Cross, Cumbria, and on a stone panel from Jarrow, Northumbria. The knotted pattern of the side panels, again a Northumbrian design of curvilinear shapes, can also be found on the East Lothian **Morham** shaft, on the cross-slab at **Glamis**, Angus, the cross-slab of **Woodwrae**, Angus, and on the stone no. 5 at **Meigle**, Angus.

The narrative front panel, however, does not belong to the Anglo-Saxon or Carolingian world into which it has so persistently been placed since the days of its discovery in the churchyard of St. Andrews. Stylistically this panel belongs to the Greek-Scythian world of the 5th to 4th centuries BC. The artist who carved this panel was well acquainted with Scythian art as it was practised under Greek influence north of the Mare Pontus. Greek realism prevails in the features of men. The long straight nose and heavy brows, prominent ears, the hair piled up on top of the head, seen on the lower figure in the middle of the panel, have an almost archaic Cretan touch about them. Such faces occur again on gold and silver coins circulating in Gaul and Italy in the 3rd and 2nd centuries BC. The elongated features of the main figure to the right of the panel betray Celtic characteristics, a resemblance to Celtic busts of La Tène times; those of the 'God of Bouray' from St. Germain-en-Laye, and of the Lady of Elche, Alicante, of 400 BC, for instance.

The man wrestling with the lion is too sturdy for Greek taste, he has however assumed a Greek stance: he is leaning heavily on his left foot, while the right leg is turned back and the front of the right foot lightly touches the ground. His carefully draped garments are of a Greek style. Scythians were fond of reproducing the cascading folds known from figures on Attic vases of the 5th century BC.

The same figure also shows Mesopotamian influence. The heavy curls of the hairstyle originated from Assyrian fashion and were used to characterize a king or hero. That this heroic figure should appear twice in the telling of a tale on the same panel betrays a Sumerian style, where the narrative duplication was also used for the purpose of balance and symmetry. In typical Greek manner the same hero is mounted on a prancing horse which is too small in proportion to the rider; such horse and rider imagery is often shown in Scythian art: we have only to think of the famous golden comb surmounted by a fighting scene, from the Solocha *kurgan* (Dnieper) of the 4th century BC (St. Petersburg, Hermitage), and of similar sturdy little horses with cropped manes reproduced on Scythian and Celtic torques, such as the Celtic gold torque

THE SARCOPHAGUS OF ST. ANDREWS

terminals from the princely tomb at Vix (Côte d'Or) of the 6th - 5th century BC (Châtillon-sur-Seine, Musée Archéologique) and the Scythian gold torque terminals from Kul-Oba (Crimea) of the 4th century BC.

34

34 Two Scythians on kneeling horses

How important this narrative scene must have been during Pictish times may be realized when we look at the slab no. 3 at **Meigle** where an artist of a later date has copied the shaggy little horse and the rider in a similar position from the scene on the St. Andrews sarcophagus. We can also trace the very original formation of the St. Andrews' horse's tail to its twin: the tail of the horse ridden by the goddess Epona on a later Celtic stele of the 2nd century BC, now in the Rheinisches Landesmuseum, Bonn.

35

36

35 Pictish horseman

36 Epona on horseback

Of Celtic origin is the shape of the scabbard worn by the largest figure, terminating in identical decorative metal scrolls turned upwards, found on many Celtic scabbards from the 5th to the 3rd centuries BC. The wave-like design on the sheath was often employed in the 5th century BC and shows the influence of Iranian bronzes.

The curvilinear 'vegetal style' of the background foliage has oval leaves and there can be no doubt that the plant represented

37

is the mistletoe (*viscum album*, the most common of a genus of sixty or seventy species); its slightly pointed leaves are symbolically used with Celtic masks and faces. They have healing qualities and are associated with the idea of a renewal of life, and with the god Esus. We are reminded of the La Tène design on the Irish Turoe Stone (Co. Galway), of the leaf pattern on the sophisticated Celtic gold parade helmet from Agris, Charente, of the 4th century BC,[1]

38

and of the background of a 4th century BC gold headdress in the Greek-Scythian style from Kul-Oba, Crimea, where simple leaf patterns are intermingled with palmettes and lotuses.

37 Pfalzfeld column.
A Celtic menhir with mistletoe foliage

38 Top part of Greco-Scythian cylinder headdress

It is difficult to decide whether the rider is carrying a quiver on his left side. The Scythian *goryt* was always carried on the left, but the actual position on the Sarcophagus relief seems to incline the quiver towards the front and not, as would be correct, towards the back of the warrior. It does however seem to be a quiver and its division into decorative panels, as indicated on the relief, would fit with the style of a 4th century BC Scythian *goryt*.

    The liveliness of the animals, the aggressiveness of the lion, the prominent outlines of the ribs, all reveal a Greek-Scythian style and an earlier Urartian influence, as seen on the Greek-Scythian *omphalos* plate of the 4th century BC from Solocha. The lean hunting dogs are of Greek breeding and we find them again on Greek, Eastern Aegean and Scythian work, such as the Greek *metope* with Artemis and Actaion from Doric Selinus, Sicily, of the 5th century BC, on a fragmented bowl from Klazomenai, a town on the western coast of Asia Minor,[2] and on the Scythian gold relief of a stag resting, from Kul-Oba, Crimea, of the 4th century BC.

39

40

39 Lions attacking horses and stag:
detail from *omphalos* plate (Scythian)

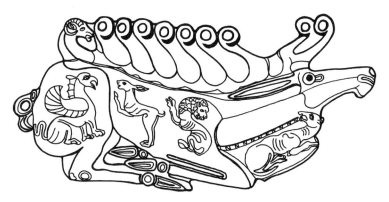

40 Stag resting with dog:
Shield emblem (Scythian)

The presence of Urartian and north Iranian influences is also confirmed in the depiction of the lions. The snub-nosed profile and the wide open mouth of the attacking lion, the circles marking his fur, the rounded ears, are typical of the 7th century BC 'ringlet' style of Urartu, originally derived from Assyrian sources. And just as a Ziwiyeh lion would have had, the St. Andrews' king of beasts also shows parallel lines running down between nose and upper jaws. The spiral terminating the body of the lion-eagle in the lower part of the panel again represents the 'ringlet' style and so do the tails of the lions terminating in rosette or bud-like shapes. The vertical lines emphasising ribs on the bodies of the dogs and of the lion to the right of the panel go back to the style of Urartu, Ziwiyeh and Luristan.

41

42

41 Lion (Ziwiyeh)

42 Lion (Urartu)

A closer scrutiny of the St. Andrews front panel will take us even further, into the realm of gods: on the top left hand side we find a 'sun wheel' design, often associated with the weather god of Urartu, Teisheba. And equally subtle, interwoven with the background foliage, but unmistakably placed on to the back of the attacking lion, we discover a *triquetra* sign, identical to the one a Hittite queen once raised in adoration in front of an altar. (We shall deal with the importance of this sign in Part IV, chapter 3). It does not therefore come as a surprise when we discover a rosette on the left haunch of the largest lion. This was *43* not only the trademark of lions from Urartu, Ziwiyeh and Luristan, it was also shown on Assur lions of the 9th century BC as a sign belonging to the Assyro-Babylonian goddess Ishtar, the goddess of war and fertility, closely linked to the sun. She was associated with lions in her warring capacity and her astral character, the Venus star, was symbolised by a rosette.

43 Lion (Luristan)

Chapter 2

The Epic of Gilgamesh

The narrative scene on the front panel of the **Sarcophagus of St. Andrews** has always been wrongly interpreted. It does not show 'three images of David, based on the Old Testament story',[3] a statement so often and erroneously repeated, when the Sarcophagus is assigned to early Christian art. The story told on the front panel is that of the great epic hero Gilgamesh, the ruler and 'shepherd king' of the ancient town of Uruk in southern Mesopotamia. Many versions of the Gilgamesh epic exist and it is helpful to take a look at history to arrive at a better understanding of their origins.

The historical Gilgamesh has been placed into a time between 2750 and 2600 BC, when the early post-diluvian dynasties of the Sumerians reigned over southern Mesopotamian towns and part of Babylon. The Sumerians were an ancient people who had moved into the delta area of the Tigris and Euphrates during the 4th millennium BC. Originally they might have come from Iranian highlands or from eastern or even northern Asiatic mountain country. Their predilection for high places, artificially erected hills and temple towers (the ziggurats), the adherence to godly images on mountain tops and their archaic timber built houses, could not stem from people of the plains. Sir Arthur Keith concluded that: 'one can still trace the ancient Sumerians eastwards among the inhabitants of Afghanistan and Baluchistan, until the Valley of the Indus is reached, some 1,500 miles distant from Mesopotamia.'[4]

The Sumerians brought with them a corpus of law, a system of numbers and astrological observations, and a cuneiform (wedge-shaped) system of writing. Their language was extinct by 1800 BC, but by then Sumerian culture had extended its influence over the whole of the Mesopotamian world. The 'learned' language of the Gilgamesh texts was still being used long after the Sumerians had been conquered by the Semitic tribes of northern Mesopotamia.

By 3000 BC Semitic nomads had moved north from Arabia into Palestine, Syria and Mesopotamia. Like the Celts, the Semites were not a race of people but a group of tribes with related languages derived from a common root.[5] After 2000 BC the Semitic Akkadians merged with the Sumerians and much of northern Sumeria as well as part of Elam in south Iran came under Akkadian control. Mesopotamian city states continually clashed and conquered each other's territories. Internal evolutions or external pressures, disputes over land and water supplies, rivalries stemming from economic success and trading, encounters between nomad and farming groups, all played their part. Eventually, at about 1760 BC the Akkadian Babylon under Hammurabi (1792-1750 BC) achieved the leading rôle amongst the southern Mesopotamian cities.

During the ethnic upheavals of the 18th century BC, or even before, Hurrian people (who did not speak an Indo-European language) had moved into northern Mesopotamia. They were eventually ruled by the Mitannians, who created an independent kingdom which reached in the west almost to the Mediterranean and in the east as far as the northern Zagros mountains. The Mitanni stayed in power until ca 1350 BC, when the kingdom of the god Assur (who replaced the Sumerian god Enlil) assumed the leading rôle in Mesopotamia as Assyria. Mitannian rule, which included an Indic element in its culture, had united northern Mesopotamia with Syria and had established links with the culture of the Indo-European speaking Hittites in western Anatolia. Assyria remained culturally dependent on southern Mesopotamia. Babylon was considered the centre of learning which supplied northern scribes with the literary and religious texts of the south.

At about 2100 the last Sumerian dynasty of southern Ur had experienced a cultural renaissance during which many myths were written down and older documents copied out. The Semitic Akkadians translated part of the Gilgamesh story into the Akkadian language, but the Akkadian versions often differed from those of earlier Sumerian texts. Unfortunately little has come down to us of the Old Babylonian texts of 1800-1600 BC.

At a very early time the Gilgamesh legends must have spread over many parts of the Middle and Near East and we encounter them again in north Mesopotamian Hurrian lands and west in Anatolian Hittite country. Excavations near Boghazköy in Anatolia brought forth fragments of several clay tablets from the archives of a Hittite king written in Hittite language as well as fragments of clay tablets in the Hurrian language. We are therefore faced with a variety of tablets in different languages and interpretations. Our main source of the Gilgamesh story, however, goes back to the 12th century BC when a poet from Gilgamesh's original home town of Uruk (the biblical Erech) created the epic poem we now know. The poem was copied by scribes in the following centuries and these copies have come down to us mainly from clay tablets in the great library of the Assyrian king, Assurbanipal (ca 669-627 BC), at Niniveh. Further fragments of tablets from the 6th century BC have been found in Babylon. In 612 BC Niniveh was razed to the ground by a combined assault of Scythians, Medes and Babylonians and the clay tablets of the Gilgamesh cycle lay buried under the rubble of the once famous library until they were re-discovered in the 19th century AD.

The Gilgamesh epic has survived mainly in four languages: Sumerian, Semitic Akkadian (consisting of Old Babylonian and related Assyrian languages), Hittite and Hurrian. There are also incomplete Canaanite and Palestinian versions. The written traditions went of course side by side with oral traditions. If we take into account that this story had existed from a time in the third millennium BC to the 6th century BC and that it has still not lost its impact on the modern reader, then we must acknowledge an extraordinary literary achievement, unique within the cultural traditions of cuneiform writing, and one of the great epics of world literature.

Chapter 3

The Story of the Epic

In archaic times the town of Uruk was famous for its size. It extended over an area of about 5.5 square km. The town did not cover all of this, vast spaces had been left free to accommodate people and their herds in times of stress, for the whole town was surrounded by a great wall. The builder of this wall was their king Gilgamesh.

Like so many rulers of antiquity Gilgamesh is of godly demeanour. He is two parts god and one part man, for his mother was a goddess and his father, king Lugalbanda, is semi-divine. Gilgamesh is tall of stature, courageous, of a creative spirit but also restless of character, since he is torn between a human and a divine world. Constantly looking for new hurdles to take, his energy becomes a menace to his townsfolk. Shamash, the god of the sun and divine judge, is his protector, and from the beginning Gilgamesh sets out to achieve immortality for himself. Later in the epic he rejects the approaches of Ishtar, who is not only the goddess of love, but also a warlike goddess fond of battle and not to be trusted in her affections.

For the sake of a fighting contest between two men, so appreciated in antiquity, a strong man from the wilderness is brought to Gilgamesh. Both look forward to this fight and both are caught in appreciation of each other's valour. This admiration turns into friendship and love. Enkidu, the wild man, becomes Gilgamesh's servant and close friend. The whole epic is indeed a great hymn to friendship. The love Gilgamesh extends to Enkidu eventually breaks down the inner harness of unapproachability he has set around himself and he begins to care deeply for another human being.

Enkidu himself has grown up in the company of wild animals. He is often portrayed covered in hair — half man, half bull — or as a centaur; a wild ass was his father and a gazelle his mother. He is endearingly called the 'swift ass of the mountains' and the 'panther of the steppe' by Gilgamesh.

Enkidu's protector is the god Enki (Akkadian Ea), one of the creators of mankind, the god of the subterranean fresh water ocean *(abzu)*. Enki is associated with magic and incantations, his elements are the sweet, life-giving waters, and he is sometimes called the 'stag of the *abzu*'. In his rôle as the creator of the animal world he is the exponent of primitive wisdom who enjoys tricks, subterfuges and is occasionally not without malice. Enki's temple *44* was called the 'house of water' and the god is often portrayed sitting in his shrine surrounded by streams of water and by small fish swimming along the flow.

44 Enki in the watery *abzu*

Against the counsel of the elders and disregarding *45* unfavourable omens Gilgamesh and Enkidu set out together to conquer an 'evil' spirit, a giant watchman over a cedar forest.[6] On their journey to the forest Gilgamesh is beset by dreams, but Enkidu interprets them as favourable prophesies. The quest of the two heroes seems successful. They kill Humbaba (Sumerian *Huwawa*), the watchman of the cedar forest, and Enkidu builds a large door out of chosen wood which was then floated down the Euphrates *46* to be offered at Nippur to the temple of the mighty god of winds and storms, born of the union of heaven and earth, Enlil. But Enlil is not pleased with the killing of the guardian of the forest who is also a nature divinity. Moreover, the two friends have enraged *47,48* the goddess Ishtar and killed the Bull of Heaven she has sent out against them. There is a council of the gods. Shamash, the sun god, is reproached for having dealt with the friends as 'his equals'. Shamash manages to protect Gilgamesh but the gods decide that Enkidu has to die in punishment.

45 Seal with Gilgamesh and Enkidu

46 Enlil or Adad, his son

Both Enkidu and Gilgamesh had betrayed their respective worlds. Enkidu, by joining mankind had turned against the spirit of the wilderness. He had revealed the existence of the watchman and taken part in his slaying. Gilgamesh, although himself of godly descent, had slain the Bull of Heaven and insulted a goddess. He had also failed in his combined function as king and priest. The throne of kingship and the activities of a priest were closely linked in Sumerian and Assyrian times: the king, as protector to his people, was in charge of the 'life force', and the voice of this 'life force' could be heard in the sound of the ritual drum. We read in Tablet 12 that Gilgamesh had dropped the drum and the drumsticks and lost them to the Underworld.[7]

The last part of the epic deals with the great grief of Gilgamesh after the loss of his friend. He is almost mad with sorrow, he turns to the wilderness in search of his own immortality and he questions the whole of human existence. His desperate journey takes him to mountain passes, where he sees lions playing in the moonlight. Gilgamesh kills the lions and comes to the mountain of the sun.[8] The guardian to the realm of Shamash, the sun god, is part man part dragon with a scorpion's tail. He permits Gilgamesh to pass through the gate and after many leagues' journey underground in dense darkness Gilgamesh emerges on the other side of the mountain into the garden of the sun by the shores of the great Ocean into which flow the waters of death. Gilgamesh is determined to cross the Ocean but the sun god tells him that 'no mortal man has gone this way before, nor will, as long as the winds drive over the sea.'[9]

47 Ishtar 'dressed to kill'   48 Ishtar in astral aspect

Gilgamesh is then told by a shaman woman who brews intoxicating drinks and lives on the shore at the edge of the sea how to find the ferryman to take him across; she also warns him that the acceptance of life and not the search for immortality should be his aim. The ferryman and Gilgamesh cross the waters of the Ocean, but the journey is not without peril for, before meeting up with the boatsman, Gilgamesh, in a rage, had smashed images of stone which stood in the woods by the shore and which were used to help towards a safe crossing. We do not know what these holy images were but are told that the ferryman was busy with *Warane*;[10] and *Warane* must be the Vedic god Varuna, Enlil's Indian counterpart, whose functions overlap with Vayu, the Vedic god of winds. Enlil was the supreme god of atmosphere, wind and storms, and one of the holders of the tablets of destinies. He was also Gilgamesh's opponent and it is doubtful that he would have provided 'a favourable wind' for the crossing of the Ocean. It is likely that the magic stones smashed by Gilgamesh were images sacred to the worship of Enlil. A small ivory image of ca. 150 BC found in the Oxus district in southern Tadzhikistan may provide a clue to the mysterious holy stones. A winged figure, a hybrid creature with a snake-like fishtail and the forelegs of a horse, holding an oar in the left hand and the symbol of the sky (or the earth) in the right hand, comes near to Varuna's *makara* symbol.[10]

49

49 Fantastic sea creature from the Oxus

By using long poles the ferryman and Gilgamesh succeed in crossing the last part of the Ocean into which flow the lethal waters of the river of death. The guardian of the far shores, the 'Faraway One'[11] who knows the secrets of the gods, tells Gilgamesh about the plant of immortality. It is a prickly plant, hurtful to the touch and comparable to a rose or to holly, which Gilgamesh manages to retrieve from the sweet underground waters. But during his journey back to Uruk he loses the plant to a snake which can therefore shed its skin and renew itself. Gilgamesh returns to his kingdom, and his human predicament, unsolved, becomes once more clear, for the cycle ends with his own praise for the wall he built around his town. His immortality will not be greater than that of any heroic personage.

Chapter 4

The Interpretation of the Front Panel of the Sarcophagus of St. Andrews

Pl. 1
Once we are acquainted with the story of Gilgamesh and Enkidu the front panel of the **Sarcophagus of St. Andrews** reads like a page out of an old book whose meaning has suddenly become clear.

In a very subtle way the artist has created a division in the visual field and the action develops to either side of it. The great stream of events which carries men and animals towards the left side is initiated by the kingly figure on horseback of Gilgamesh. IIis long hair with large curls is typical of the Assyrian and Near Eastern Gilgamesh style. A falcon, the emblem of royalty, is sitting on his left hand. He brandishes a sword and strikes out at a lion which has already risen against his mount. Below the rider is Enkidu. He is slightly ahead as he had promised to the counsellors of Uruk in order to protect the king on the journey to the cedar forest. Enkidu was called the 'wild ass of the mountains' and that he is doomed as such is shown in the scene enacted between the small horse of the steppe and the attacking griffin. In a dream shortly before he was to die, Enkidu had felt an enormous creature descending upon him, in the likeness of the bird of heaven, *Anzû*, with lion's claws and eagle's talons, who trod him down like a wild animal and encompassed his whole body and carried him off to the House of the Dead. The gazelles which flee before the party of men and dogs seem to repeat the feeling of panic. Riding upon the hind quarters of one of them and looking back

50 towards the men is the figure of a sphinx; she represents the spirit of death already prevailing in the mind of Enkidu, the vision of the Underworld where, according to the epic and Semitic sources, such

50 Scythian sphinx

80

creatures are dwelling: 'They are clothed like birds, with wings for garments, and see no light, residing in darkness.' [12]

The sun wheel formed by the branches of mistletoe above signals trouble.[13] It is the wheel of Heaven but, as Heaven's executive, the god of thunder, Enlil, is also associated wih the fiery wheel. And Enlil aims at destroying the two friends. The hooded figure amongst the branches of the forest is a nature spirit, perhaps the spirit of the forest guardian himself.

The direction of the stream of movement sweeping men and animals towards the left hand side of the narrative scene is perhaps no coincidence. Mesopotamian reliefs tended to locate the losing parties to the left of a scene; the left side implied a connection with the other world, with chthonic elements and, sometimes, with bad luck. In contrast, the tall figure of Gilgamesh wrestling with a lion is turned to the right. He is subduing a lion on his way to the mountain of the sun. The damaged squatting figure behind him is the guardian of the gates to the mountain, half monster half man with the — still discernible — scorpion's tail. Finally, the ram between the two images of Gilgamesh represents the dynastic line; according to the Sumerian king-list Gilgamesh was descended from the Sumerian god Dumuzi (Tammuz in Hebrew language), a god of vegetation, and a shepherd. Gilgamesh's ancestor and protector, king Lugalbanda, was also a shepherd, as had been all kings of the early post-diluvian dynasties.[14]

51

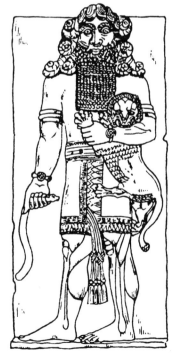

51 Gilgamesh: an Assyrian relief

Chapter 5

Narrative Scenes of Early Christian Times

To the Picts the story of Gilgamesh must have represented the great legend of their forefathers, the epic of a hero involved with the gods. That this epic is carried right up into Christian times may have given rise to the confusing and bewildering interpretations of scenes which have always been forced into a Christian context, but which could never be satisfactorily explained. Pictish crosses incorporated Anglo-Saxon and Scandinavian styles and their relevance will be examined in Part V. We will limit our research into Pictish imagery in Part II of this book by attempting further interpretations of Pictish stones concerned with the old Sumerian legend or with later Romano-Celtic descriptions of gods (such as Epona).

52   With the exceptions of earth spirits and gods of chthonic connotations, Cernunnos or the great Earth Mother, the highest Celtic gods tended to be abstractions and their presence was disguised in abstracted designs or hidden behind masked images. Only under Roman influence did Celtic gods become 'visible' and the *locus consecratus*, the open air Celtic place of worship mentioned by Caesar, became a temple, a theatre, a votive shrine or a pilgrims' hall. Diodorus Siculus vividly illustrates this fact in his account of the sacking of Delphi by Celtic tribes in 279 BC. Their commander, Brennos, is said to have burst into loud laughter when, on entering a Greek temple, he was not only faced with gods in human shape but with the fact that they were, moreover, also 'imprisoned' in a building. Just as Scythian art only showed the human figure when Greek influence prevailed, Pictish nature religion had not encouraged the representation of gods as men, but had instead shown their symbols. These symbols continued to be used, combined with the Christian Cross, which in itself has an abstracted quality about it.

52 The Pictish Cernunnos
Part of **Meigle** Stone no. 22

We are admittedly faced with the question why the ancient story of Gilgamesh should have been so enthusiastically revived during Christian times. The Christian insistence on the human figure, the many representations of saints and scenes from the Saviour's life, Christ in Majesty, for instance, trampling the lion and dragon, must have greatly encouraged the Picts to create a visual evidence of their own mythical heroes. What we see on the back of early cross-slabs or combined with the crosses on the front are therefore not scenes from biblical stories, but scenes from Pictish mythology.

Pl. 4   The stone of **Meigle** no. 2 (back of cross-slab) shows a large central figure with out-stretched arms, flanked by four lions.

53 Great Goddess with animals.
From a steatite vase, from Khafaje (Iraq)

53

Such a gesture by the Great Goddess, whose divine vitality pervades nature, can already be traced back to the Early Dynastic Period of Sumer (3000-2340 BC). This theme was later taken up in Assyrian art and had spread from the banks of the Euphrates and the Tigris, as the image of the 'Master of Animals', to the Hurrian lands of the Mitanni in north-west Mesopotamia, to the Semitic Aramaean people of northern Syria and to the Hittites of Asia Minor.

54
109

We find this theme again in the 7th-8th century BC west Iranian bronzes of Luristan. It was well known in the east and in the later classical world as the 'Gilgamesh Motif'. It is a heraldic group of a warrior with rampant lions, his arms raised in a position which comes near to the 'orans position' repeated in the early European Middle Ages, but which had originated several thousand years before in the east as a gesture of worship. It is also a theme repeated in the Christian story of Daniel in the Lions' Den and Scripture scenes often show the number of lions increased.

54 The Master of Animals, Luristan

The scene of **Meigle** no. 2 may imply a merging of the biblical story with the ancient epic of Gilgamesh, but it is quite clear that the 'pagan' version remains the stronger element in the narrative. We can still distinguish the Assyro-Babylonian style in the frontal posture of the Pictish 'Master of Animals', in the position of the shoulders and the slightly awkward angle of the arms in relation to the chest. The headdress in particular may even be traced back to much earlier Neo-Sumerian times. Another 'Master of Animals' with his beard trimmed in a straight line and a fringed robe may

55

be seen in a 9th century BC statue in the Assyrian-Aramaean style of Sam'al in northern Syria.

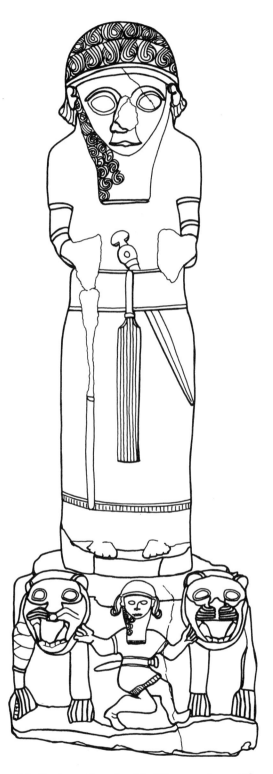

55 Statue of god with Gilgamesh motif
on base, from Sam' al

The Enkidu of this panel is represented in a classical myth-ological context as a centaur, half horse half man. In Mesopotamian mythology the centaur may be shown as half horse or half lion and half man. The figure of the bull-man or the bull with a human head corresponds astronomically to part of Centaurus, and the bull-man was a common theme during the period of the historic Gilgamesh. The etymological meaning of the name of centaurs signifies 'those who round up bulls'.[15] Enkidu is brand-ishing two axes in front of the branches of the cedar woods. We cannot come to a definite conclusion about the figure to the lower left of the panel, but there might be a possible resemblance to a nature spirit, such as that of the **Rhynie** Man, a rather crude carving found in the Rhynie area of the Grampian,

56 The Rhynie Man

45

56

now displayed in Woodhill House in Aberdeen. The two animals engaged in a fight which terminate the scene at the bottom of the panel, leave no doubt that we are indeed looking at the story of the old epic: the monster which is attacking a bull and is about to win the contest comes very near to the eastern image of an Indian *makara* [16] (or Chinese *bixie*), a zoomorphic creature which has risen from the depth of the earth and the waters and represents the forces of nature. It is therefore a complex monster combining good and bad qualities; Indian images sometimes show the *makara* with waterplants emerging from its mouth, a symbol of fertility.

57

In the Mesopotamian pantheon the *makara* is the snake-dragon of the god Enlil's executive, in older traditions his son, the god of storms Adad. On Mesopotamian seals Enkidu is often represented as half man, half bull; the scene on **Meigle** no. 2 thus symbolizes the victory of the god Enlil over Enkidu, the nature-man represented by the bull. (This bull should not be confused with

Ishtar's 'bull of heaven' which could also be associated with the storm god.)

57 Neo-Assyrian snake-dragon
with scribal god Nabû

The riders above this scene on **Meigle** no. 2 are the companions of the two friends setting out on their journey.[17] Their horses repeat the Greek style of the horse of the **St. Andrews Sarcophagus**. The sphinx to the left of the panel has assumed a hybrid aspect between a bird and an angel.

Pl. 5

58

Repetitions of scenes from the epic of Gilgamesh also occur on the back of the cross-stone **Meigle** no. 1. The panel is very badly worn but we can still distinguish the riders setting out, the winged being to the left, and a very typical *makara* or water dragon on the lower right. Displayed above the scene are the symbols and the *triquetra* sign of the gods who prevailed over man's final destiny.

58 Indian *makara* — water dragon

Pl.6   The back of the cross-slab by the roadside at **Aberlemno** has been said to show, on the left, the figure of David as a warrior carrying a shield, repeated and doubled up in the image, on the right, of two trumpeters, and then repeated again on the lower panel grasping the jaws of a lion.[18] Since the party on horseback comes so near to the Gilgamesh scene already described and is setting out under very forceful and impressive symbols placed above the men, it is hardly likely that a hunting party would warrant such a display of heavenly omens. The two heralds on the top right sounding their fanfares may well be calling an assembly as the Lord had demanded of Moses.[19] But we must not forget that trumpets made of one piece, the mouth small, nearly a cubit long, and the end funnel-like, were of very ancient Asian tradition and design, so that the use of trumpets does not necessarily warrant a biblical story. Below the riders the shepherd king is subduing a lion and we cannot doubt that he is Gilgamesh, since to the left of the panel the centaur-like Enkidu is carrying off a tree from the cedar woods and he certainly does not do this to fill an unwanted space, as has so often been proposed.[20]

The back of the cross-slab at **Elgin** has prominent symbols above and riders below. The lower part of the stone has been broken off and the weathered conditions of the existing relief scenes do no longer allow for a clear interpretation.

173   On the cross-slab at **Glamis** Manse the 'illustrations' are placed on the front panel, around the arms of the cross, and we see from left to right, moving clockwise: two men of an equal giant stature engaged in a deadly contest. The man on the left bears great similarity to the **Rhynie** Man; he also seems to be the losing party, since his oppressor on the right has established a firm grip on his wrist and is brandishing a battle axe above his head. The next scene shows a cauldron out of which hang the legs of two victims. The epic tells us that the vanquished Humbaba was torn asunder by the winning party and presumably thrown into a cauldron.[21] The giant of the woods was not alone but had a servant with him who was also killed by the two friends.[22] The Pictish cauldron which contains two pairs of legs thus fits the story. Dismemberment of a victim to prevent the enemy's return from the dead was not unusual in antiquity. Above the fighting scene with the cauldron is the image of a griffin, a combination of the eagle and the lion. As a magically protective creature the griffin, like the sphinx, is thought also to relate to the Underworld in Mesopotamian religion. The image of the griffin probably originated in Syria in the second millennium BC. The top field on the right side of the **Glamis** cross holds the image of the centaur Enkidu brandishing two axes. The last panel shows the solar drum or mirror relating to the sun god Shamash and to the goddess Ishtar; the head of an antelope or a gazelle, above, recalls the mourning words of Gilgamesh after the death of his friend:

> 'The wild ass and the gazelle
> That were father and mother,
> All long-tailed creatures that nourished you
> Weep for you . . .'[23]

174   The **Cossans** stone or St. Orland's Stone, as it is traditionally known, is standing on a hill surrounded by marshland which was once open water. Riders are again setting out under the now damaged symbols of the gods. This time their direction is from the left to the right of the scene. On the lower panel we see a boat — the only boat known on a Pictish slab. It has a high prow and stern, there are probably five people in the boat and we can still distinguish a rudder and oars. A large object is being transported in the barge. On the scene below a hybrid monster has gripped the horns of a bull; the fishtailed creatures which frame the back panel repeat the theme of the chthonic water monster and thus establish an obvious link to rivers and waterways.

The symbolism of the contesting creatures on the lowest panel may again be related to the story of Enkidu, the bull-man, being vanquished by Enlil's *makara*. We are immediately led to search for further proof of a re-telling of the ancient story. The strange, bulky object transported in the boat has a certain familiarity about it: if we turn to the Gilgamesh epic we read that, after vanquishing Humbaba, Gilgamesh singled out a particularly high pine and out of this choice wood Enkidu — whose patron, the god Enki, is also the patron god of carpenters — made a large door 'six poles high and two poles wide, its doorpost is a cubit . . .'[24] This door was destined for the temple of Enlil and floated down on river ways, probably on the

Euphrates, to the town of Nippur. Mesopotamian architecture was massive and arcuated, and arched doorways were typical of the Sumerian style.[25] The door which Enkidu built already had the importance of a shrine about it, for no stranger was to approach it and only the god himself was to pass through. From Sumerian literature and Akkadian cylinder seals we know that statues of gods made ritual journeys in boats. 'During that period of Mesopotamian history when each year was named after an important event of the preceding year (about 2300-1650 BC), the refitting and caulking of the boat of a god was a sufficiently grand and expensive undertaking to serve as a year-name.'[26] The raised setting of the **Cossans** stone and its surrounding waters thus becomes a very appropriate place for the boat of a god and its divine journey.

Pl. 7   The lady portrayed on the **Hilton of Cadboll** stone should not be interpreted as the main figure taking part in a hunting scene. She is not a Pictish 'lady of the manor' enjoying an outing with her hounds. We should not read this scene with eyes and mind conditioned by medieval tapestries, as has so often been the case when Pictish stones are described. Pictish monuments were created to honour gods and, in a higher sense, to express the metaphysical ideas and ideals which must have served to encourage the very reasons of tribal existence. The lady in question is the Great

Goddess herself. She is the Akkadian Ishtar or the Sumerian Inana but, riding side-saddle, she has undergone a Roman metamorphosis: she has become the goddess Epona, so popular in Romano-Celtic times when the great Celtic goddess of war, of fertility, the Goddess of Plenty and the protectress of the dead as well as of the living, had her attributes curtailed and her actions limited to those of the 'mother' of horses and pack animals.

59

59 Epona from Alesia

90

When reducing Epona to a stable goddess Rome was already applying a westernized logic to a theme far removed from its original Eurasian sources. Buryat (southern Baikal area) legends tell us that the horse was considered the purest of animals and the most pleasing to the gods; the god of the sky, thunder and lightning could appear in the clouds in the shape of a stallion. His consort, the goddess of fertility, could appear as a mare. In Romano-Celtic times the Great Goddess was also known as Sequana, the personification of healing springs.

Pl. 7 The **Hilton of Cadboll** stone was badly weathered, and subsequent cleaning while in museum care has tended to smooth over the soft surface of the sandstone. The faintly incised lines on the horse can, however, still be made out in old photographs (e.g. plate 31 in the booklet *St. Ninian's Isle Treasure*, published in 1981 by the National Museum of Antiquities of Scotland). One can discern the

60 sign of the snake-goddess and the sign of the battle-axe on the haunch of the horse, as well as the weather god's dagger sign.

60 The Great Goddess on horseback
Detail of **Hilton of Cadboll** stone

61 The combined signs of the battle-axe and the snake goddess may also be seen on an Iranian bronze *situla* from Luristan, of the 7th century BC, where they have been incorporated into the design of the legs supporting a royal bed.

61 Part of a bronze *situla* from Luristan

The Ishtar nature of the lady is also indicated by her headdress which appears to bear horns and a floating band, in Levantine and north Syrian manner of the first millennium BC (as may be seen, for example, in figure 142); her hairstyle may be compared with that of the queen in figure 61. On her headdress we see the rosette, the emblem of the Great Goddess, similar to rosettes set around figures or faces on Luristan bronze pin-heads.

60   The Great Goddess on the **Hilton of Cadboll** stone is also holding the head of a war-axe in front of her; it is not a brooch fastening her cloak, as always stated.

62   On the lower panel of the Pictish stone we recognize once again the symbol of the snake goddess, decoratively stretched out and combined in a pattern of many scrolls. Enclosed within these scrolls is a triangle, a *triquetra* sign.

62 Lower panel of **Hilton of Cadboll** stone

Indo-European and Celtic mythologies have various godly triads, fundamental constructions of religious experience. We are at liberty to make our own choice when explaining the triad of the Great Goddess: Sequana, under yet another name, that of Rigani, was associated with the Celtic god of regenerative earthly forces — Esus or Cernunnos — as well as with the god of heaven and thunder — Taranis or Teutates — and the triad Esus-Rigani-Taranis is well known.[27] The triad of the Great Goddess may also be explained with reference to her three functions, as Queen of Heaven, Goddess of War and Goddess of Fertility.

The lady in the side-saddle has her warring symbol, the mirror or sun disc set before her and Ishtar's prancing lion behind her. The second rider — we can discern the legs of his mount which have the same rhythmic movement as those of the lady's horse — also has his symbol set before him: a strange object in relief on a block, very much in the shape of blacksmiths' tongs. A similar image is also known from Hittite seals, meaning the *li*, the weather god's dagger.[28] The dagger image is in turn related to the two-pronged thunderbolt of the Mesopotamian weather god so that the lady's companion may well be the storm and weather god himself, the Celtic Taranis or Teutates. The two riders could thus symbolize the union of Earth — in the person of the Mother Goddess — with the Sky — in the image of the god of Thunder.

The Great Celtic Goddess, like her Mesopotamian counterpart, the goddess Ishtar, is a lady of many names and many husbands and should also be mentioned under her Romano-Celtic name of Rosmerta, a fertility goddess who may hold a snake, a horn of plenty, or fruit, but also (as on a stone relief from the Shakespeare Inn, now in Gloucester City Museum) a double-sided war axe. She can also have a ring-staff identical to the reed rod shown on Sumerian seals and pottery.

63 Rosmerta with axe-staff, and Mercury

The fertility goddess is also related to the image of the stag. In Celtic as well as in Sumerian mythology the stag, renewing its antlers, represented the earth cycles. To the Celts the very shape of the antlers combined the female vulva and the male phallic symbols. The Celtic myth of Rigani and Cernunnos uses the sacrifice of a stag to ensure anew the beginning of life in Spring, and the hunting of the stag on the **Hilton** stone may be seen as representing a cyclic sacrifice. The lady's long curly hair relates her to the Irish *Flidais*, the woman with the beautiful hair, who, as the 'mistress of the stags', resembles the Celtic Diana and is also the mistress over life and death, the Great Mother Goddess.[29]

The figurative panel of the **Hilton of Cadboll** stone set under a 'firmament' of heavenly symbols and framed by yet another Indo-European fertility symbol of birds and plants, far from being merely a pleasant hunting scene, sums up the essence of Pictish beliefs, so close to the Pictish people and the Pictish warrior. From the stones which have survived, it seems that such complex figurative representations only arose fairly late in Pictish history and under the stimulus of Northumbrian art and of another religion: Christianity.

64, 65   The **Migvie** stone repeats the martial theme of the Hilton stone in the chain links incorporated into the cross, in the image of the two approaching riders and in the precise, incised lines of the weather god's dagger. An identical dagger point and a similar dagger have been found in Denmark; the dagger executed in bronze, the dagger point in flint, both copies of older oriental weapons and dated between 1500 and 1300 BC.[30] The symbols of the gods are closely fitted into the fields of the cross arms above, and a last reminiscence of the Great Goddess's fertility theme is to be seen at the base formed by the graceful curves of two snakes.

64 front — **Migvie** Stone — 65 back

178   The damaged and re-shaped cross-slab no. 7 at **St. Vigeans** has a relief panel composed of several *triquetra* signs at its base. Ascending the shaft of the cross are the 'earth signs' of the Great Goddess, followed by further abstracted designs embodying the Celtic sign of the sun wheel, which seems to have been repeated on the now missing top part of the cross. The figurative images on either side of the cross shaft imply three sacrificial scenes: to the left a man is being held upside down ready to be immersed in a *162*   cauldron. A similar scene is seen on the Gundestrup bowl and it is known that the Celts sacrificed their victims to Teutates by drowning them in large vessels. A second sacrifice to the right of the stone is that of a bull, its blood being received by the man kneeling in front of the victim. The third sacrifice is also that of an animal, probably of a wild boar held up between two seated figures.

Georges Dumézil in his monumental studies explains such sacrifices as being known in Vedic Indian times: the three superior sacrifices then were those of a man, of a horse and of a bull. The man was sacrificed to the highest god, the horse to the god of war and the bull to the gods of fertility who, in Vedic times, were twins representing the life of the farmer and of the shepherd.[31]

Already during Hallstatt times the wild boar had become the symbol of the Celtic warrior class to such an extent that the boar, in his fierce fighting moods, became allied to Teutates himself. It is therefore very likely that the third sacrificial victim at **St. Vigeans** to the spirit of war is not the horse but a wild boar.[32] The three sacrifices thus explain the triad signs which, in the case of **St. Vigeans**, must relate to the god of the sky, the god of war and the (twin) gods or the goddess of earth and fertility.[33]

177   The stone of **Dunfallandy** repeats the theme of the ideo-logical triad on the back panel. A small cross, centrally placed and flanked by two seated figures, creates a division, left and right. This top scene is 'ruled' over by the abstract 'heavenly' images we associate with most Pictish stones, and which we will discuss in Part III of this book. The lower panel lends itself to be interpreted in martial terms: a rider, possibly Teutates himself, is set above a hammer, an anvil and a sign which is reminiscent of blacksmiths' tongs. Hammer and anvil were used to forge weapons and war was fought in the name of the god Teutates, the 'father of the tribe'. Teutates and Mars, the Roman god of warfare, were often linked and their names fused into one as is the case with the latin title *Marti Toutati* found on a silver votive plaque in Hertfordshire.[34] The weather god Taranis — *taran* means thunder — is also associated with Mars, and Teutates and Taranis have interchangeable qualities.[35] Both gods, when in a war-like mood, wield a hammer, and the Teutates/Taranis myth combines the image of the godly father, the *Dis Pater* of the tribe, with that of the war and weather god. Thus the 'tongs' shown with the hammer and anvil can be seen in yet another dimension, as two lightning forks. In Celtic mythology hammer and lightning symbols as well as the war axe were sometimes carried by the same god.[36]

176 On the **Dunfallandy** front panel elongated *makara-* like creatures, symbols of earth, water and fertility, as well as a life-like stag, are placed on either side of the shaft of the cross which stretches belt-like through the stone. The angels on the right hand side with four wings each, two of them pointing downwards, have

66 had Assyrian forefathers and are direct descendants of a winged genius of Neo-Babylonian origin. A parallel image also occurs on a Phoenician or Syrian stele where it represented a fertility god.

The angel with drooping wings on the front of the roadside cross-slab at **Aberlemno** may therefore be seen as a magically protective fertility figure, holding, not a book,

156 but a square vessel similar to those on Mesopotamian reliefs, where genies carry the elixir of life.

66 Winged genius on door jamb, Pasargadae (Iran)

NOTES TO PART II

1   The Irish Turoe stone is described and illustrated in *The Celts*, Venice exhibition catalogue, 1991, *op. cit*., p. 616, as is the Celtic parade helmet from Agris, *ibid*, pp. 292-3

2   For the Greek metope with Artemis and Aktaion, from Temple E at Selinus, see G. M. A. Richter, *A Handbook of Greek Art*, London, 1959, fig. 132 on p. 99. The bowl from Klazomenai is described and illustrated in the catalogue *Aus den Schatzkammern Eurasiens*, Kunsthaus, Zürich, 1993, ill. no. 75 and pp. 154-5

3   A. Ritchie, *Picts*, Edinburgh, 1989, p. 40

4   Quoted in C. W. Ceram, *Gods, Graves and Scholars*, London,1954, p. 216
    The first Semitic empire was founded about 2300 BC by King Sargon.

5   'The absolute chronology of Mesopotamia is not established.
    For periods after 2100 BC, errors are unlikely to exceed one century.
    For the period 3000-2100 BC, allowance should be made for errors of about two centuries. Before 3000 errors of several centuries become increasingly likely and cultures and periods frequently overlap.'
    Quoted from Julian Reade, *Mesopotamia* , London, 1991, p. 70

6   The cedar forest has historically been placed in the Lebanon or in the Zagros mountains; it could equally be the pine forest of Amanus in southern Cappadocia. It was probably situated north or north west near the upper Euphrates. Wood was a valuable commodity in those days and could be floated down the rivers to the southern towns of Mesopotamia.

7   Tablet 12 of Sumerian origin is a later addition to the eleven Tablets of Babylonian origin, and a shamanistic summing up of the epic.
    The poem tells us that the drum and the drumsticks had been made out of a tree where a snake lived among its roots, a female demon in the trunk and the eagle of Shamash, Anzû, in its branches.

8   It was a Sumerian belief that at sunset the sun god would descend into a western mountain and then travel underground to emerge again at sunrise from an eastern mountain. The mysterious link between lions and the moonlight may be explained when we realize that lions were sacred to the goddess Ishtar, who aimed at destroying Gilgamesh and Enkidu. Ishtar is the Great Goddess and her functions are complex, since she can appear as a warring as well as a fertility goddess. According to varying traditions Ishtar can be the daughter of An (Heaven), but also the daughter of the moon god (Sîn) and the sister of the sun god (Shamash). She was also regarded as the daughter of Enlil or even of Enki. Another interpretation saw her as the wife and sister of Enlil. In one of her aspects Ishtar is the goddess of love and temple prostitution. As a fertility goddess she may be linked to the

moon god who presides over the cycles of life and death. Her astral aspect is the planet Venus and her usual symbols are the star or the rosette. Another aspect of Ishtar is that of a fierce warlike goddess who rides through the sky in a chariot drawn by seven lions.

9   N. K. Sanders, *The Epic of Gilgamesh*, London, (1960), 1972, p. 100

10 (i) Mention of *Warane* occurs in the translation by A. Schott, revised by W. v. Soden, *Das Gilgamesch-Epos*, Reclam, Stuttgart, 1958, 1988, p. 83. *Warane* is close to *Uruwana*, meaning Varuna, as mentioned in the treaty of about 1380 BC between the rulers of the Hittites and Mitanni, translated in J. B. Pritchard, *Ancient Near Eastern Texts*, Princeton, 1955, pp. 205-6

    (ii) Binding things are mentioned in connection with the stones, translated as 'the tackle of the boat' by N. K. Sanders, *op. cit.*, p. 104, as 'strings' by S. Dalley, *Myths from Mesopotamia*, Oxford, 1989, p. 104, and as 'chains' by A. Schott, *op. cit.*, p. 86. These may refer to the magic binding forces of Varuna, mentioned by M. Eliade, *Images and Symbols*, Princeton, 1991, chapter III.

    (iii) N. K. Sanders, *op. cit.*, mentions '*urnu* snakes', after J. B. Pritchard, *op. cit.*, pp. 91 and 92, which would make sense in connection with Varuna's *makara*, the snake monster of watery domains. The word *waran* is associated in the Akkadian Dictionary by W. von Soden - *Akkadisches Handwörterbuch*, 1959-81, vol. 3, pp. 1431-2, with *urnu* I. According to this dictionary, *ur-nu* can also mean 'yellow-green', and *urnû* is tentatively translated as 'mint (?)', *ur-nu-ú* as 'drug'. If one could interpret 'mint (?)' as 'mistletoe' one could establish a link between Varuna, the *urnû* plant and the mistletoe plant of the Celts. (See note 13).

    (iv) 'Wings' and 'breast' are mentioned in connection with the images of stone in D. J. Wiseman, 'Additional Neo-Babylonian Gilgamesh Fragments to Akkadian sources,' published in *Gilgames et sa légende*, P. Garelli (Ed.), Paris, 1960, pp. 128-31

11 N. K. Sanders, *op. cit.*, p. 105

12 S. H. Hooke, *Middle Eastern Mythology*, London, (1963), 1991, p. 52

13 In Celtic mythology, mistletoe leaves are associated with the gods Esus, Teutates and Taranis. The obovate mistletoe leaves were believed to have healing powers and to induce fertility, and they were carefully cut with a golden sickle from trees on certain nights by Celtic druid priests, a ritual which was accompanied by the sacrifice of a white bull. The symbolic value of the mistletoe plant was also seen in its evergreen colour and in the fact that the mistletoe did not grow on the ground but on certain trees, 'between heaven and earth', and best near water, which may explain the association of the plant with snakes. (See note 10. iii). It is seen in combination with heads and masks. Mistletoe leaves grow in opposite pairs and illustrate the

Celtic principles of opposing forces, which are also indicated in Janus heads. (See also S. and P. F. Botheroyd, *Lexikon der Keltischen Mythologie*, Munich, 1992, pp. 107-9, 173-5, 235-6.)

14 Traditions of herding in Mesopotamia went back to a time of about 10,000 - 6000 BC, which is often called the Neolithic revolution.

15 *New Larousse Encyclopaedia of Mythology*, London, 1968, pp. 161-2

16 In pre-Vedic times the Indian god Varuna (Enlil's nearest equivalent) was the highest god, linked to the sun. During Vedic times he lost his position to Indra and became the god of waters; overlapping functions with Vayu, the god of winds, are apparent. Varuna's vehicle is the water monster, the *makara*, with the head of an antelope and the tail of a fish or a snake. Vayu's vehicle is the antelope. The *makara* is also explained in Part III, ch. 4, p. 127

17 In the Sumerian poem *Gilgamesh and the Land of the Living*, found on 14 tablets at Nippur, one at Kish, and two of unknown provenance, all dating from the first half of the second millennium BC, the text informs us that Gilgamesh and Enkidu departed with fifty companions. N. K. Sanders, *op. cit.*, p. 126. See also S. Dalley, *op. cit.*, footnote no. 32, p. 127: 'In the Sumerian story of Gilgamesh and Huwawa, citizens of Uruk accompany the two heroes; but they journey alone together in this Akkadian version. In the Hittite version they travel along the Euphrates to the Pine Forest (Otten 1958).'

18 A. Ritchie, *op. cit.*, p. 27

19 Before the Exodus out of the wilderness of Sinai we have the following text, *Numbers* X, 1 and 2:
'And the Lord spoke unto Moses, saying, Make these two trumpets of silver; of a whole piece shalt thou make them: that thou mayest use them for the calling of the assembly, and for the journeying of the camps.'

20 e.g. A. Ritchie, *op. cit*., p. 27, and I. Henderson, *The Picts*, London, 1967, p. 142

21 A. Schott, *op. cit*., p. 51. Translation of Tablet V, lines 11-15. Tablet V from Uruk is damaged in parts. Line 13 mentions the cauldron.

22 A. Schott, *ibid*, p. 48, Tablet of Uruk, II, line 3; also pp. 52-3, Old Babylonian tablet.

23 N. K. Sanders, *op. cit.*, p. 94

24 S. Dalley, *op. cit.*, Gilgamesh V, p.77. We know that during the Late Assyrian period doors to temples moved on huge pivot shafts and were equipped with heavy hinges. A late Babylonian Gilgamesh version mentions a huge door with huge hinges.

25 The arch in building was introduced into Europe by the Romans. It had been unknown in the Western world until Greek architects, following the conquests of Alexander, began to evolve this new method

of building. Hittite architecture in Anatolia was making use of this style around 1360 BC, where the base of the archway is broader than the top part.

26   J. Black and A. Green, *Gods, Demons and Symbols of Ancient Mesopotamia*, London, 1992, p. 45

27   Just as in Indian myths the highest pre-Vedic god, Varuna, eventually develops overlapping functions with Indra, the Aryan god of wind, thunder and of war, so do Esus and Teutates in Celtic beliefs have overlapping functions, a fact which greatly complicates Celtic studies. Esus may be equated with the Roman Mercury but also with Mars, and Teutates can be Mars but also Mercury. See S. and P. F. Botheroyd, *op. cit.*, pp. 107-8 and 326-8

28   E. Akurgal, *Die Kunst der Hethiter*, Munich, 1976, p. 40

29   S. and P. F. Botheroyd, *op. cit.*, pp. 84, 127, 160, 162. The Ephesian Diana/Artemis is referred to in Part IV, ch. 4, p. 160 and in Part V, ch. 1, p. 189

30   J. Brøndsted, *Nordische Vorzeit*, volume II: *Bronzezeit in Dänemark*, 1962, ills. pp. 15 and 17: dagger from Fur and dagger point from Serup, Fünen.

31   G. Dumézil (after L. Gerschel), *L'idéologie tripartie des Indo-Européens*, 1958, p. 29

32   S. and P. F. Botheroyd, *op. cit.*, pp. 94-5

33   The Vedic twin gods were the Ashvin or the Nasatya.

34   Seven silver plaques, with the largest inscribed *'Marti Toutati'*, together with a bronze statuette of Mars, were found in Rockywood, Barkway, Hertfordshire, and are now in the British Museum.

35   S. and P. F. Botheroyd, *op. cit.*, pp. 322-4 and 326-8

36   S. and P. F. Botheroyd, *ibid*, the hammer god Sucellus, pp. 313-5

* * *

PART III

Gods and Symbols

Chapter 1

The Universe

The Greeks who based their mythology on eastern sources retained the story of the Mesopotamian Creation Myth amongst their own tales. The Greek myths were later re-told by the Latin poet Ovid who turned to Latin folklore and to Babylonian and eastern sources and then gave a superb account of the newly born world as antiquity saw it. In his great lyrical epic *Metamorphoses* we read:

'Before there was any earth or sea, before the canopy of heaven stretched overhead, Nature presented the same aspect the world over, that to which men gave the name of Chaos. This was a shapeless uncoordinated mass, nothing but a weight of lifeless matter, whose ill-assorted elements were indiscriminately heaped together in one place. There was no sun, in those days, to provide the world with light, no crescent moon ever filling out her horns: the earth was not poised in the enveloping air, balanced there by its own weight, nor did the sea stretch out its arms along the margins of the shores. Although the elements of land and air and sea were there, the earth had no firmness, the water no fluidity, there was no brightness in the sky. Nothing had any lasting shape, but everything got in the way of everything else; for, within that one body, cold warred with hot, moist with dry, soft with hard, and light with heavy.

This strife was finally resolved by a god, a natural force of a higher kind, who separated the earth from heaven, and the waters from the earth, and set the clear air apart from the cloudy atmosphere. When he had freed these elements, sorting them out from the heap where they had lain, indistinguishable from one another, he bound them fast, each in its separate place, forming a harmonious union. The fiery aether, which has no weight, formed the vault of heaven, flashing upwards to take its place in the highest sphere. The air, next to it in lightness, occupied the neighbouring regions. Earth, heavier than these, attracted to itself the grosser elements, and sank down under its own weight, while the encircling sea took possession of the last place of all, and held the solid earth in its embrace. In this way the god, whichever of the gods it was, set the chaotic mass in order, and, after dividing it up, arranged it in its constituent parts.'[1]

In Mesopotamian cosmogony the goddess Nammu, a personification of the primeval freshwater ocean, whose name is written with the ideogram for *abzu* or 'sea', united herself with a snake-dragon, Tiamat, a monster who lived in the salt-water ocean. It is said in myths that 'their waters mingled' and out of this union came the gods, including those of heaven and earth.

Some myths also tell us that heaven and earth originally formed one mountain. Earth was its base and heaven at its summit. Heaven was personified by the god An (Akkadian Anu), and earth by the goddess Ki. Out of their union came Enlil, the god of air and atmosphere, who then separated heaven from earth thus creating the universe, in the form of heaven and earth linked by air. Enlil is thus the supreme god of Creation, the ultimate source of life on earth, of vegetation, of agriculture and eventually of civilization, and the holder of the tablets of destiny. He is helped in his activities by lesser gods who carry out his instructions and are therefore closely related to him.[2]

Enlil is the 'god who binds', for not only did he separate heaven and earth, having done so, he 'bound' them together by the intervening air. 'The Babylonian word *markasu*, "link, cord", means in the mythology, "the cosmic principle that unites all things", and also "the support, the power and the divine law that hold the universe together". '[3] As the god of winds Enlil transmits the breath and word of Anu himself. But just as air and clouds are made up of watery elements, so does Enlil's cosmogony extend from the atmosphere of the sky to the water on earth, and he belongs to a chthonic as well as to a lunar stratum. Enlil controls the powers of life and death. His 'bonds' imply spiritual as well as warlike forces.

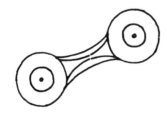

67 **Aberlemno** linked discs   68 **Golspie** linked discs

The Pictish symbol of two discs linked together is the supreme triad of three gods: of An or Anu (god of heaven), of Ki (earth) and of Enlil (god of wind and atmosphere).

67, 68
69

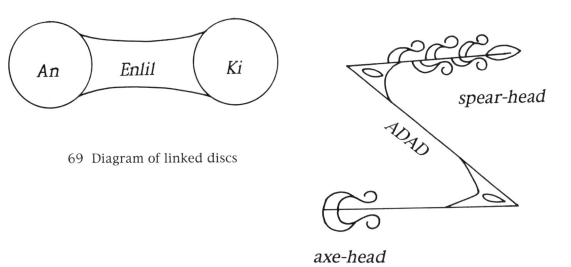

69 Diagram of linked discs

spear-head

ADAD

axe-head

70 **Dunnichen**: Adad,
god of war and storms

70 The Pictish symbol includes yet another sign, that of the rod of lightning. Indo-Iranian mythology never limited the nature of gods to one characteristic function but allowed for overlapping, and sometimes opposing, elements in their make-up. Enlil, as the supreme spirit, is also linked to warlike forces, and the god of war, whose lightning symbol we see, is closely associated with him. The Mesopotamian god of war is Adad, a weather god, symbolized by the rod of lightning and the thunderbolt. Adad is his Akkadian name; in Syria, Phoenicia and Canaan he is Hadad. Adad was usually regarded as the son of An. According to an older tradition he was the son of Enlil and, as he embodied the power both of storms and war, he was also the executive of Enlil. The central

69, 73 element in the diagram of the Pictish symbol implies a linking of two forces: that of Enlil's cosmological plane, a magico-religious

71, 72 world, crossed by the lightning symbol of Adad.[4]

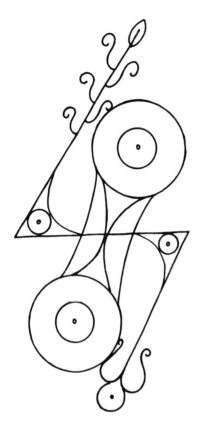

72 **Dunnichen:**
double discs and lightning rod

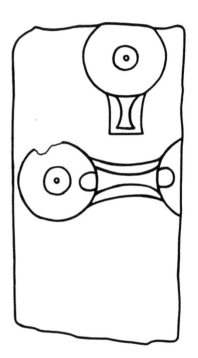

71 **Aberlemno** roadside:
double discs and lightning rod

73 The 'bonds' of Enlil on symbol stone
from Westfield Farm, **Falkland**

The Pictish discs with central points or circles are reminiscent
of the Greek-Scythian *omphalos* (navel) plates. According to
Mesopotamian tradition man was fashioned at the 'navel of the
earth'.[5] If we recall the spiritual importance of the central pole, or
the shaman's 'Tree of Life', the Pictish symbols become quite clear:
they indicate the sacred core or central opening, the narrow door
or the spiral ascent and descent, turning (in a positive or negative
sense) between heaven, earth and the Underworld, the symbolic
centre out of which man was born.

In archaic times man was closely linked to cosmic forces. Metaphysical metamorphoses between animals, plants and men, and a transition from the world of gods to life on earth were not unusual. A Mesopotamian hymn in praise of Nergal, god of the Underworld, has the following lines:

> 'His eyes were Enlil and Ninlil,
>   Sin is the pupil of his eyes,
>   Anu and Entu are his lips,
> . . . His ears are Ea and Damkina,
>   His skull is Adad . . .'[6]

74 Southern Siberian rock engravings of about 3-2000 BC show human masks with 'cosmic features'. They provide an almost perfect illustration to both, the Mesopotamian poem and Pictish symbolism.

74 Incised image on stone from Tschernowaja, Siberia

Chapter 2

War

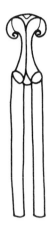

75 Axe-head on plinth: **Dunrobin** symbol stone

76 Axe-head on plinth: **Abernethy** symbol stone

The Pictish symbol which — through lack of better interpretation — has always been described as a 'tuning fork' is in fact a supreme symbol of war. It is the image of a battle-axe placed high on a plinth or an altar. Such axes in the shape of a half moon with elongated flanges were known during Bronze Age times in Inner Mongolia. They are reproduced on Iranian rock carvings and are known to have existed in Susa, Elam, at the beginning of the second millennium BC. As part of a chariot or horse gear they assumed a symbolical meaning in Persepolis, and as ritual axes they were depicted in Indian art. They have been excavated in Palestine and Luristan, used during the mid-second millennium in Hungary and western Georgia, and they are related to the Koban-Colchian axes of a later date with less pronounced flanges from northern Ossetia. The Celts reproduced them as parts of horse gear or as a symbolic shape to a linchpin. In Bronze Age rock pictures from Bohuslän, Sweden, they are being held up by warriors in a ritual boat. They were indeed already being used during Early Bronze Age times in Scandinavia. Two such axes have even been excavated on the Scottish site of Gavel Moss, Renfrewshire, recovered from a hoard which probably dated from the middle of the second millennium BC.

75, 76

77

78

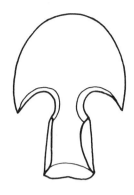

77 Axe-head from Akhalkalaki
south-western Georgia

78 Axe-head from Gavel Moss

75, 76   The plinths on which these axes are standing seem to be Pictish copies of metal steles. Curiously enough such steles may be seen in China amongst the bronzes of the 'Six Dynasties', the 'Sui Dynasty' and the 'Tang Dynasty' where, in a shortened version, they formed bases to display Buddhist images. Like the Pictish plinths the Chinese stands can be straight, but we also know examples of the side supports designed in curvilinear lines, similar to Pictish design. In southern Mesopotamia up to the 7th century BC large boundary
79, 80 stones (*kudurrus*) show symbols of deities on similar plinths or altars.

79 Mesopotamian boundary stone
(detail)

80 Temple and altar on
Middle Assyrian seal impression

111

Another note may be added to this evidence of cultural exchanges between East and West when we consider a southern Siberian rock carving of the 15th-11th centuries *81* BC depicting a mask-like face displayed on what is most probably a metal plinth.

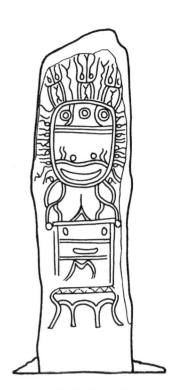

81 Incised mask image on plinth from Yenisey

We are inclined to misinterpret the motivation of archaic warfare. 'Because they attack, and endanger the equilibrium and the very life of the city (or of any other inhabited and organised territory), enemies are assimilated to demonic powers, trying to reincorporate the microcosm into the state of chaos: that is, to suppress it.'[7] An enemy is therefore always 'evil', and fighting occurs against demonic powers and is helped by the blessing of the gods. The war axe shaped like a half moon may thus be understood as invoking the protection of the moon god, whose light would show up demonic forces active during the night. In Mesopotamian mythology Sin, the moon god, rises above the head of the god of war.[8] Moon cycles could also represent alternating periods of creation or destruction. In the Hinduistic pantheon, Shiva, the god of creation and destruction, carries the half moon in his headdress. An interesting parallel to this theme is given in the tale of the boyhood deeds of the Celtic hero Cú Chulainn. The saga tells us that as a boy, when Cú Chulainn was overcome by his battle rage, 'the warrior's moon rose from his head.'[9]

A good example of the 'spirit of battle' raised on to a high construction is found in Herodotus' description of the Scythian ceremonies in honour of the war god whom Herodotus mentions under his Greek name of Ares. The temple of Ares, he states, 'is of a peculiar kind, and consists of an immense heap of brushwood, three furlongs each way and somewhat less in height. On top the heap is levelled off square, like a platform, accessible on one side but rising sheer on the other three . . . and on the top of it is planted an ancient iron sword, which serves for the image of Ares. Annual sacrifices of horses and other cattle are made to this sword, which, indeed, claims a greater number of victims than any other sacrifice of animals'. Herodotus then continues to explain how human sacrifices of prisoners of war were also made to this sword.[10]

82 Warrior moon with axe-head designs: **South Ronaldsay**, Orkney, symbol stone

83 Warrior moon with axe-head designs on **Logie** and **Lynchurn** symbol stones

82, 83
84
The great ritual significance of the Pictish battle axe may be reconstructed in the curvilinear designs incised into the Pictish half-moon symbols, just as the end parts of the fiery rods which cross over moons and snakes and plinths are no chance decorations, but are again stylized images of the axe-head. The symbol of the war axe is the emblem of a great god. On a higher level of thinking — which had its active outcome in sacrificial ceremonies — its blades could cut the bonds of ignorance and free men of earthly ties.

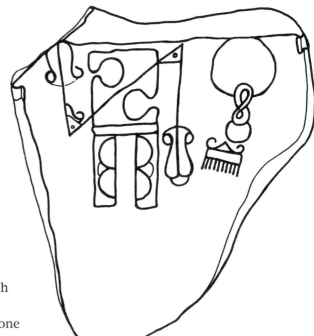

84 Notched altar or plinth
and lightning rod:
Clynemilton 2 symbol stone

Further symbols of war may be detected in the 'boomerang' shapes — half circles or half horseshoes — such as the one shown on *85, 86* the stone of **Strathpeffer**. We know of an interesting parallel in Shaiva cults, when the spear of the god of war was said to return to his hands much in the same way a boomerang would have done. Such throwing devices, already used by Stone Age man in Europe, were known in southern Asia and in Asia Minor where they were also appreciated for their sound. The Gaelic name of the Strathpeffer 'Eagle Stone' was *Clach Tiompan* or 'Sounding Stone'.

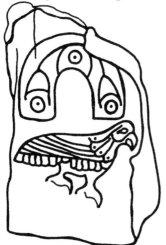

85 **Strathpeffer** stone
with 'boomerang'

86 **Clynemilton** 1 stone
with 'boomerang'

175

Pl. 7

87, 88

The mirror as a sun disc is the symbol of the Great Goddess, but we cannot be so sure that all Pictish images so far taken as mirrors were not also meant to reproduce sound. Visually the mirror and the gong are very near to each other. Some Pictish mirror images are clearly discs with movable rings attached on one or two sides. Such constructions could also belong to drums hung from supporting frames, as they are indeed still being used by Asian nomads.

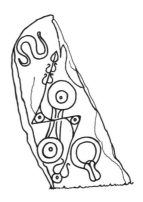

87 Mirror-gong with head of antelope: **Glamis** Manse cross-slab

88 **Aberlemno** roadside symbol stone, with mirror-gong

93

The mirror gathers and holds light, there is a 'magic' quality about it which the shaman has recognized, for he compares the reflections of light to reflections of thought. The highly polished surface of a gong or copper drum not only reflects light but also sound. The sound of the drum represented the primeval world and the first elements of life. We must not forget that 'speech' to archaic people meant the utterance of 'truth', since original sound could not be other than genuine.

89

The sound of the drum must also be thought of as Pictish war music. Drums and drumsticks were made of perishable material and did not survive the ages. A long wave-like object may have been a drumstick and this deduction is not quite as speculative as it may seem, since modern Tibetan *Cham* dancers of the Bon tradition still use similar drumsticks.[11]

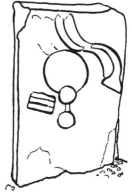

89 Wave-like object and mirror-gong **Drimmies** symbol stone

90, 93   The Pictish mirror and comb image has always been used to settle any doubts that the two belong together and serve to improve a lady's looks. But combs have been found in Scythian warrior graves as frequently as they have been discovered with female burials. Indian mythology teaches us to value the comb as a symbol of status and an elaborate hairstyle can be of fundamental iconographical importance, designating the qualities and virtues of the wearer. Hairstyles may be so richly ornamented and piled up so high on the head that they become crowns, and in Hindu mythology it is not possible to distinguish between an actual crown or hair pinned up high and worked into an elaborate pattern, as the crown and the hair-do merge into each other. Gods are recognizable by the style of their headdress and the same godly personality can wear different hairstyles according to the spiritual aspect which dominates at a given moment. In archaic societies the hairstyle of the men could be an indication whether the nation was at war or at peace. When Scythian chieftains prided themselves on neatly trimmed hair and beards their vanity also reflected their status in society. The Picts were a nation of warriors and

Pl.5   we feel justified in assigning the symbol of the comb in the first place to the warrior rather than to his lady.

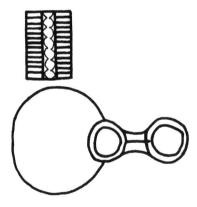

90 Mirror or drum with comb
on **Dunrobin** symbol stone

79   Mesopotamian boundary stones depict the symbols of gods: images of the sun and the moon and of the star-rosette, but also of animals belonging to the gods. Heads of rams, goats, bulls, horses and lions, as well as the water monster, are raised into prominent positions on steles. Similar animal symbols of deities were also

116

represented in the headdresses worn by dignitaries of state as an insignia indicating rank, rights and prerogatives. South Iranian rock reliefs of Sassanian times provide us with valuable illustrations. The relief of Darab[12] shows men in the retinue of the king wearing Phrygian caps, already known in Asia Minor by the 8th century BC. A juxtaposition with the Pictish diagram on the **Golspie** slab leaves no doubt that on the Scottish stone we behold a cap very similar to the Phrygian type placed on a stele: an image very near to any symbol of state raised on standards, staves and sceptres.

91

92
179

91 Cap of dignitary
Darab relief, Iran

92 Cap on stele
Golspie cross-slab

93

The so-called 'flowers' or 'lilies' placed high on the **Dunnichen** stone are equally likely to be the picture of a cap, whose tassels seem to end in battle-axe shapes.

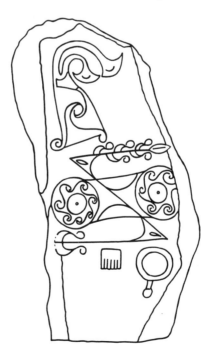

93 **Dunnichen**
symbol stone

94   A small bronze sculpture of an Iranian horseman wears a cap topped
      by the head of a duck. On a south Iranian rock relief from Bishapur
95   an Iranian dignitary displays a lamb-headed headdress.[13]

94 Cap with duck's head
worn by an Iranian nomad

95 Lamb-headed headdress
    Bishapur relief

96
Pl. 5
87
173

Pictish caps topped by animal heads may be seen on the back of the cross-slab of **Meigle** no. 1 and on the front of the cross-slab at **Glamis** Manse. We have already associated the head of the 'gazelle' at Glamis Manse with Enkidu from the Gilgamesh epic (Part II, chapter 5). The link with the god Enlil and the position of the headdress close to the mirror-drum image give it a ritual connotation. Enlil's Indian counterpart is the god Varuna, who rides on a sea monster (*makara*) whose head is that of a gazelle or antelope. (For the *makara*, see also Part II, note 16, and Part III, chapter 4, page 127).

96 Animal head on cap:
Meigle no. 1, back

97

Two silver plaques from **Norrie's Law** show the inlaid heads of two beasts. They are typical representations of headdresses with side ornaments, in this case the fertility symbol of the Great Goddess.

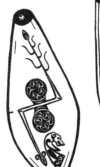

97 **Norrie's Law** plaques

It is tempting to apply a shamanistic interpretation to the Norrie's Law plaques. The lightning rod crossing between heaven and earth and descending on to the image of a cap topped by the head of a beast, a hound or a lion, implies yet another dimension, that of the Underworld, into which Ishtar descended during the barren period of the year.

98   The stone of **Papil**, Shetland, transmits a similar linking of three worlds: an early Christian cross or Tree of Life has taken the shape of its crown from four stylized axe-heads. A knot is set into its lower trunk and beneath it we see a lion or a huge dog. In Mesopotamia the lion was an attribute of the warrior goddess Ishtar who, during yearly fertility rites, ascended again from the Underworld. The Celtic equivalent of this Ishtar myth may be found in the story of the warring and fertility goddess Rigani. A lion, with upright ears, demon-like, was associated in later Assyrian and Neo-Babylonian times with the figure of a 'smiting god', which could occasionally afford magic protection. In a Celtic sense, the animal may be seen as a dog rather than a lion. The Celts were known to have very big dogs and in Celtic mythology the dog was considered to be a messenger between two worlds, who would guide the soul of the dead to the 'other' world and again to a new life on earth. The two men on the Papil stone, below the animal, bearing shaman's masks of water birds and holding up a skull with their beaks, have certainly 'descended' into a subterranean realm.

98 Stone of **Papil**, Shetland

Chapter 3

The Ideology of the Three Functions

In order to appreciate the significance of 'war' in Indo-European thinking we have to consult the research of two scholars, Georges Dumézil and Stig Wikander. Based on S. Wikander's conclusions on Vedic and pre-Vedic influences in Indian mythological elements, G. Dumézil evolved his theories on the three religious and social functions within the Indo-Iranian and Indo-European ideologies.[14]

Before outlining the basic elements underlying the division of Indo-Iranian society into three ideological groups we should be aware of the fact that such tripartitions were not rigidly employed, and that they varied according to the nations and the people who may or may not have followed such a scheme. Indeed, according to Dumézil, such tripartite divisions may not have gone beyond being merely ideal solutions in many Indo-Iranian societies. But, at the same time, if the ideal of the three functions remained a hidden element in social structures it still provided valuable means by which to explain the mythical and religious forces which formed the Indo-Iranian and the Indo-European worlds.

The first and highest function within a social group is that of the sacred law, which is at the same time the highest spiritual element pervading the world. In Indo-Iranian religion two gods shared this function, the Indic gods Mitra and Varuna. Mitra personifies the supreme law-giver, and the friend and protector of mankind. Varuna is the more mysterious ruler who can be menacing and is responsible for punishments; he employs magic forces and is armed with a sling, and 'the wind is his breath and the stars are his eyes'. Both gods 'see' and 'shine': Mitra, the Sun, during the day; Varuna, the Moon, during the night.

The second function, that of warfare, is represented by the god of war, Indra. Indra works under the intoxicating powers of the sacrificial liquid *soma*, the drink of the warrior, also called the moon liquid. Indra represents the necessity of brutal force, he is the fighter of demons and the saviour of the universe.

The third function is represented by twin Indic gods, the Ashvin or the Nasatya, who work for the prosperity derived from tending the fields and the herds. They stand for fertility, the production of riches and material goods and the pleasures of this world.

The Indian caste system of the three *varnas* , the three social classes, consisting of the class of the king and priests (*bráhmanas*), the class of the warriors (*kshatriyas*) and the class of the labourers, herders and cultivators (*vaishyas*), is another expression of the three functions seen in a sociological context. Such class divisions, applicable in India, are however not always clearly traceable in other Indo-Iranian domains.[15] Varying patterns are constantly at work and it is in this sense that Dumézil explains the many variations in Celtic, Roman and Scandinavian developments of the old Indo-Iranian religious themes.

Herodotus (IV, 5-6) relates how the Scythians described the origin of their nation: The first man, Targitaos, the son of Zeus and of a daughter of the river Borysthenes had three sons... 'and during their reign in Scythia there fell from the sky a golden plough, a golden yoke, a golden battle axe, and a golden cup.' The plough and the yoke are the symbols of the labourer, the battle axe (together with the bow) was the national weapon of the Scythians and the cup was the symbol of cult offerings and ritual drinks.

The same ideological structure also survives in the Ossetian sagas. Their mythical heroes, the Nartes, originated from three main families: the Boriatae, rich through the possession of herds, the Aexsaertaegkatae, strong in warfare, and the Alaegatae, distinguished by their intelligence.[16]

Amongst the Celts of Gaul and of Ireland the same Indo-Iranian tripartite division takes place. The *bó airig* of Ireland are the labourers and owners of cattle (*bó*), the free men (*airig*), protected by the law, the electors of the king. The military aristocracy (*flaith*) is given to warlike functions, while to the class of the Druids belong the priests, the law givers and the 'wise men' who uphold the old traditions.[17]

All three functions are closely connected and the balance of the world depends on the welfare and right management of each of them. Thus the king (in the Mesopotamian world) may also have the duties of a priest. He has also to be a warrior, and through right administration and right sacrifices assures the goodwill of the gods and guarantees the well being of his people, of the land and of the herds.

Indra, the god of war, unites and reigns over all three functions, since land, herds, tribal culture and religion have to be maintained, and war is action closely linked to survival. In the Indo-Iranian world cattle raiding was one of the main activities of a warrior. Indra, like Varuna, is also linked to the great god of winds, Vayu. Like Vayu he rides through the sky, hurls thunderbolts and lightning rods. In Scythia and Ossetia Indra's equivalent is the great weather god of storms and war. The Aryans placed the god of war above all other gods: his angry voice was heard in the thunder and his spear seen in the flashes of lightning. Indra fulfills the rôle of Vayu and Varuna, the gods of natural elements, for Indo-Iranian religion never limited the character of any god but allowed for overlapping functions: if Mitra and Varuna are the sovereigns of the universe, the warrior god Indra — allied to several other gods such as the god of winds, the god of fire, the god of the sun — can achieve the same universal characteristics. Indra, Varuna and Mitra may all be blended into one great aspect. We read in the *Rig Veda* that the highest being is called 'Indra, Varuna and Mitra': 'He is one, (though) wise men call Him by many names.'[18] Seen in this context we have a great equation where Mitra, Varuna and Indra form one great synthesis and war is integrated as a fundamental principle in the ideology of the three functions.[19]

Following Dumézil's theories we have explained the three functions by making use of the Indian pantheon. In Mesopotamian religion, Enlil, supreme spirit and one of the creators of mankind, may be likened to Varuna. He is the god of the sling, the 'raging storm' and the 'wild bull'. According to one Sumerian poem the other gods might not even look upon his splendour. He is closely linked to the Mitraic sun principle and in later mythology he supplants Anu as the chief god.

The great Mesopotamian goddess Ishtar, whose powers reach from the heavens to the earth and to the Underworld, is linked to all the gods and we begin to understand how, according to different regions and times, she can be the wife, the sister or the daughter of the main deities. Indian philosophical speculations which see the balance of the universe as a merging of opposite forces have described the attributes of the Great Goddess as positive and negative, and she is therefore known by many names and represented as a different personage according to her varying rôles. Ishtar's warlike and terrifying powers are leonine and the theme of Ishtar's lion fighting the horse of heaven or attacking the goddess' own sacred stag illustrates the opposing elements found in all natural forces.

Chapter 4

Animals as Symbols of Transition

Every natural fact is a symbol of some spiritual fact.
Every appearance in nature corresponds to some state of mind,
and that state of mind can only be described by presenting
that natural appearance as its picture.[20]

In Pictish symbolism the transitional nature between the animal,
the human and the spiritual world is seen on the image shown on the
cross-shaft of **St. Andrews** (no. 19): two animals face each other,
their heads meet and form a new frontal combination, that of a
human face. This symbol indicating the merging of opposite forces
to form a third component was well known in the East. We meet the
same theme in the *Kui* - dragons and the *T'ao - t'ieh* masks of
Chinese Shang times. A later version combining fantasy and
realism in a 'Pictish sense' is seen on a large limestone slab from
Shantung, dated 114 AD. The figurative scenes in relief were
carved in honour of a deceased couple; man and wife, seated on
lion-like creatures, are seen riding towards each other and beating
a drum suspended between them. The heads of the animals meet to
form a human face, thus creating another dimension belonging
to a spiritual world. The Pictish slab of St. Andrews also implies
a link with the other world: the animals are accompanied by
aquatic birds and are placed beneath a shamanic initiation scene
involving two men, a young boy, possibly a drum, and the branches
of a Tree of Life.

Pl. 8

99

99 Two animals meeting and forming a single head. Shantung

100   In India the well known emblem of elephant and buffalo sharing one head is the symbol of the apparently antagonistic forces of creation and destruction combining to unite and form a central balance, which implies new creation and continuity. A Hebrew myth, 'The Hunting of Ba'al', (which may have originated in Mesopotamia), tells us that monsters with horns like bulls' could have faces like the supreme god himself. The two-in-one

101 principle was well known to the Celts: on a *situla* from north Italy two winged horses have acquired the head of an owl (the bird of the Great Mother Goddess, also connected with the Underworld). The two Celtic gods Teutates (Dis Pater) and Taranis (a warrior and weather god) can also undergo a metamorphosis showing two aspects of creation and destruction. Such a metamorphosis is

102 illustrated in two Luristan halberd blades where the head of the bird Anzû (the Sumerian Imdugud bird), the personification of an atmospheric force, resembles a Chinese *T'ao-t'ieh* mask.

100 Buffalo and elephant
     with one head. India

101 Horses sharing owl's head. Celtic

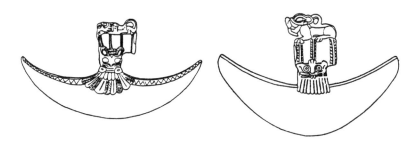

102 Zoomorphic junctures on Luristan halberd blades

From time immemorial animals served to create a bridge between higher and lower worlds. The snake, the horse, birds could all transcend planes of existence and the gods of the Indo-Iranian pantheon rode on animals whose virtues they had assimilated and whose strength they had made their own. Animals were in fact as spiritual as they were real or fantastic. The Indian *makara*, for instance, combining characteristics of many animals, served as an appropriate vehicle for Varuna and for Vayu, gods of the elements. Varuna's *makara* had the head and hindlegs of a goat or antelope, the forelegs of an elephant and the body and tail of a fish. The *makara* symbolized forces of fertility and the fundamental conception that all life came out of water and, to some extent, out of original Chaos. Thus a *makara* could vary in shape, and aspects of antelopes, lions, tortoises, fish, crocodiles, elephants and snakes could all be shown in the water monster.

182

The elephant is an animal symbol of outstanding importance amongst the Picts. In Indo-Iranian thinking the attributes of the elephant are numerous. At his best he is powerful, well balanced, radiating an aura of peacefulness and prosperity. He is also connected with the idea of fertility. There is a kinship with the snake, and the elephant comes very near to the element of 'water', the means of both physical and spiritual purification. He is often shown with the main Indian goddess of earth, beauty and happiness, Lakshmi, in a heraldic image: two elephants standing on either side of the goddess have filled their trunks with water or hold up a vessel, thus helping to bathe the goddess. Another poetic image of the elephant has him floating up into the sky where he appears as a white cloud distributing beneficial rain. As the sum total of all his virtues the elephant is the symbol of supreme wisdom which overcomes all obstacles, illusions and burdens.

26

He traverses the jungle as if it were the wilderness of Chaos and his fighting strength and determination lead to spiritual emancipation.

The elephant is the majestic vehicle of kings and warriors. The god of war, Indra, rides on a white elephant. Indian gods were associated with their vehicles and the qualities of their animals were assimilated by the gods themselves to strengthen their personalities. The association of the elephant with both Indra and Lakshmi indicates the dualism of his godly nature.[21]

In his capacity as an ascetic the Hindu god Shiva, the yogi and Lord of the Animals, is also connected to the elephant. He is depicted resting on a tiger's or elephant's skin. One of Shiva's sons is the elephant headed Ganesha, a protective and slightly playful spirit, who can remove or place obstacles in the path of people. Shaiva cults are rooted in pre-Vedic Indus Valley Dravidian traditions.

As the master of cosmic forces Shiva may be personified in a great triumphant mood (*Aghora-Murti*) performing a war dance and wearing the bloody skin of an elephant. In Tantric beliefs *103* helpful spirits in demoniacal disguise, an elephant's skin slung over their shoulders, belong to an apocalyptic world behind which hides a very advanced system of religious thinking. [22]

103 The Tantric rain god Vajrapani clad in a tiger's skin and wearing the skin of an elephant slung over his shoulders, crushing evil spirits under his feet. From a Tibetan *thangka*.

The Pictish image of the elephant may have been mis-interpreted. The so-called elephant of the Pictish stones may in fact be the image of an elephant's skin, a tribal animal symbol probably descended from Shaiva cults.

104

104 The Pictish elephant's skin
on the **Meigle** no. 5
cross-slab, left side

Almost identical designs of elephants' skins can be found in Tibetan wall hangings, in the *thangkas,* where the skins of animals are worn over the shoulders of protective deities and of helpful spirits, the *dharmapalas* and *sadhitas.* The images in Tibetan *thangkas* depict symbols of Buddhist Tantric beliefs partly based on the old shamanic Bon religion.

In Tantric thinking the skin of animals was imbued with the powers of the live creature. A man wearing a skin could assimilate the animal's strength, just as partaking of the victim's blood could enhance the life force of the victor. Ritual cleansing by blood is well known in archaic societies. Tibetan Tantric Buddhism employs the image of skins to shock us out of complacency, just as horrifying apparitions of guardians of faith are intended to frighten away the demons of daily life.

Although about 2000 BC the elephant is already shown on seals from the Indus Valley culture of Mohenjo-daro, no early representation of the elephant's skin has so far come down to us. Our main source of information is fragmentary and comes from cave paintings of the 6th and 7th centuries AD in Chinese Turkestan (Sinkiang, now Xinjiang) and from Tibetan *thangkas*, the earliest surviving examples of which date back to the 15th century AD. Along the old northern Silk Road between Tun-huang and Kashgar, in the Tarim Basin south of the Tien-shan mountains, are hundreds of caves and cave temples which once contained innumerable statues and wall paintings. Indo-Iranian and Chinese styles had merged with Buddhist teachings and over centuries these statues and paintings formed a cultural link between Indian and Chinese civilizations.[23]

105   The sketch of a protective god, Mahakala, the Great Black One, (an emanation of Shiva), sitting on a white bull and holding up an elephant's skin over his head is one of the few illustrations still available to us from which we can infer the importance of the elephant's skin in early cults.

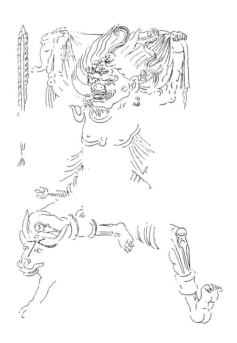

105 Mahakala on a bull holding an outstretched elephant's skin.
Cave temple of Bezeklik, Xinjiang

Such manifestations of shamanic practices must have been carried eastward from areas to the west of the Tarim Basin by steppe tribes which included the Tocharians. These people may have entered the Tarim Basin in the very broad period of between 2500 and 200 BC. [24]

Eurasian steppe shamanism and elements of Old Mesopotamian, Iranian and Indian beliefs all travelled along the Silk Roads. Buddhism must also have reached the Tarim Basin along these routes and paintings in the Maya caves at Kizil in the northern Tarim district, although dated as late as 600-700 AD, show many features of transition between the old Indo-Iranian warrior cultures and the new Buddhist faith: 'a re-evaluation of ancient shamanic motifs and their incorporation into a system of ascetic theology'.[25] We see in the cave paintings the Vedic god Indra riding on a white elephant and displaying, tattooed on his arms, the symbol of a ritual axe above a wheel; other figures in the frescoes bear similar symbols. From the cave of the Vault of the Bodhisattvas, also at Kizil, comes the painting of a Bodhisattva gutting an elephant prior to preparing his skin.[26]

It is impossible to know to what extent shamanic practices and Tantric beliefs influenced Pictish life, but we may still read into the Pictish symbol of the elephant's skin a spiritual message: the belief in the transitional nature of life on earth and the conclusion that the great cosmic forces of creation, duration and destruction arise out of the meeting and the balance of opposites.

Chapter 5

The Bronzes of Luristan

A bronze pin disc from Luristan dating from 1200-1000 BC shows the face of a mysterious god, with features half human half animal, occupying the central *omphalos* space. Beneath the god a *T'ao-t'ieh* mask illustrates the equilibrium between elements in opposition. Two men, priests, are standing on either side of the god wearing animal masks and holding palm leaves from the sacred (Sumerian) Tree of Life. The pin head is damaged and we have to concentrate on the figure on the left to interpret the scene. He wears a curious cap in the shape of a fishtail and decorated with a pattern of scales. His mask has the features of an elephant. He also wears a little goat-like beard and holds up the body of a snake. Two rosettes, emblems of the Great Goddess, are gracefully disposed between the palm leaves and seem to float up to heaven. The *makara* -like combination worn on the priest's head and the many allusions to fertility signs enable us to 'read' this scene as a ritual act to a creator god who establishes the central balance of life.

106

106 Masked priests carrying palm leaves
on bronze pin disc from Luristan

Pl. 4

The style of the priest's figure resembles that of the Pictish Gilgamesh of **Meigle** no. 2. A similar position of the arms, a similar fringed skirt, the same stance. The lord of fertility impersonated by the priest on the Luristan bronze comes very near to the Pictish Master of Animals. Indeed it is not difficult to recognize the Pictish Gilgamesh on Luristan bronzes, such as represented for instance on an early decorative plaque from southern Iran, and in order to understand the development of the Gilgamesh theme on Luristan bronzes we have to take another step back in the history of the people who inhabited the Zagros mountains.

107

107 Gilgamesh with winged animals on bronze plaque from Luristan

The inhabitants of the mountainous areas of the Zagros which lie east and south-east of the Mesopotamian plains were the Kassites. They may have been Indo-Aryans who, at the end of the 4th millennium BC, penetrated north-eastern Iran from northern Pontic-Caspian regions. Under pressure from other northern tribes they moved along the shores of the Caspian Sea and further south into the Zagros mountains. There they merged with an earlier Asian population, the Elamites, already established to the east of Mesopotamian lands.[27] During the 2nd millennium BC the Kassites succeeded in defeating Babylonia and they established a Kassite dynasty at Babylon which lasted some 500 years. At this time Sumerian and Babylonian culture exerted a strong influence on Kassite metal work. The Assyrians who subjugated the south of Mesopotamia around 1100 BC finally defeated the Kassites who then withdrew to their mountain strong-holds in those areas of the Zagros now known as Luristan.

Under Mesopotamian influence Luristan work in bronze and gold produced a realistic animal style and assimilated the human figure in the guise of Gilgamesh and Enkidu. Gilgamesh scenes were being manufactured in great numbers. The master of wild beasts developed into the kindly hunter, the protector of the shepherd and the farmer; he became the vanquisher of monsters, the guardian of humanity and a patron of fertility linked to the symbolism of the Tree of Life. Gilgamesh could be shown wearing his friend Enkidu's tiara of horns, grasping a serpent, carrying a ram or a goat or holding a pomegranate, all symbols of fecundity. He could even become 'invisible' but still present in the Tree of Life itself.

 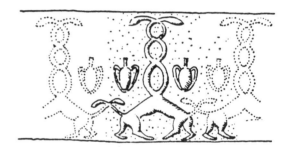

108 Sumerian seal impressions

108   The realistic Mesopotamian animal style had never ruled out fantastic animals: creatures of the imagination were still composed of realistic looking shapes taken from life.

After the Kassites had finally withdrawn from Mesopotamia the Sumerian and Assyrian inspired style began to undergo a change. Luristan bronzes became more abstracted, more refined and spiritual. Gilgamesh, the master of opposing elements, became the central

109   spine of a complex composition: the outline of this Master of Animals came very near to the shape of a human skeleton, and several planes of existence were being symbolized.[28]

109 The Master of Animals. Luristan bronze

181

182

Pl. 9,3

Similar stylistic relationships may also be detected in Pictish art. The cross-slab of **Meigle** no. 4 shows an almost 'Sumerian' realistic animal style on the front panel, and similar creatures may also be seen on the remains of the back panel and on the **Rossie Priory** cross-slab. On the front of **Meigle** no. 2 cross-slab such creatures are seen in opposition.

18

104

110,13

The later more sophisticated and abstracting style of Luristan work shows Eastern Scythian influence. There is a nomadic element of the fantastic about it. Slim elongated bodies remind us of Siberian stag stones and of mythical beasts incised on the rocks of the Baikal regions. Elongated bodies and faces, over-accentuated beak-like mouths and decorative scrolls interpret essential but not realistic qualities. It is this same style which we can almost 'feel' in the image of the Pictish elephant's skin. The curvilinear design, the flatness of the head with extended features, the large mask-like eyes, the tusks shaped like a beak, legs ending in 'ringlets' and an overall softness of line, all come very close to the style of a Luristan bronze.

110 Horse. Luristan bronze

NOTES TO PART III

1   The extract from Ovid's poem is here given in a free translation by Mary M. Innes, *The Metamorphoses of Ovid*, Penguin Books, London, 1955, pp. 29-30

2   In the Sumerian version of the Creation the god Enki, after Enlil had separated heaven and earth, fills the plain with plants and animals and places them under the shepherd god Dumuzi, who is sometimes equated with Enlil himself. Enki also lays foundations and builds houses, stables and sheepfolds, and helps to create man out of clay with the collaboration of other, minor, gods.

3   M. Eliade, *Images and Symbols*, Princeton, (1952) 1991, chapter III, The 'God who Binds'. The following footnote from the same chapter, p. 116, may also be quoted: 'S. Langdon, *Semitic Mythology*, Boston, 1931, p. 109. Several Babylonian temples are named *markas shame u irshiti*, "the Link between Heaven and Earth", cf. E. Burrows, "Some cosmological patterns in Babylonian religion" in the volume *Labyrinth*, edited by S. H. Hooke, London, 1935 (pp. 45-70) pp. 47-48, n. 2. An ancient Sumerian name for the temple is "the *dimgal* of the region"; Burrows, (p.47, Note 7) proposes to translate this "Great binding post"; *dim* meaning "post", etc. and also "rope"; probably *dim* = "to bind, thing to bind or to bind with".
The symbolism of "binding" would here be integrated into a greater whole which might be called the "Symbolism of the Centre" (see above, pp. 41 ff.)'

4   M. Eliade, *ibid*, p. 110: The 'binding' seems to be a magico-religious enchantment on an equal footing with all the other religious 'forms'.

5   M. Eliade, *ibid*, pp. 41-47

6   Quotation mentioned by S. H. Hooke, *Babylonian and Assyrian Religion*, London, 1953, p. 34

Enlil	=	supreme spirit
Ninlil	=	his consort
Sin	=	moon god
Anu	=	god of the sky
Entu	=	his consort, also goddess of fertility
Ea	=	god of sweet waters and of the earth, also god of wisdom. (Ea is Akkadian for the Sumerian Enki).
Damkina	=	his consort

7   M. Eliade, *op. cit.*, p. 38

8   The moon rising above the head of gods is illustrated in Mesopotamian cylinder seals.

9   J. Gantz, *Early Irish Myths and Sagas*, London, 1981, p. 136

10 Herodotus, *The Histories*, IV, 60-65

11 The Tibetan Bon religion was the shamanically inclined early religion of Tibet, reformed in the 8th century AD by the Indian teacher of Tantric Buddhism, Padmasambhava.

12 Deutsches Archaeologisches Institut, Teheran, *Iranische Denkmäler*, Vol. 6, 1975

13 *Ibid*, Vol. 10, 1981

14 G. Dumézil, *L'idéologie tripartie des Indo-Européens*, Brussels, 1958, and *Mythe et epopée I*, 'La terre soulagée', Paris, 1968; S. Wikander, 'Pandavasagen och Mahabharata mutiska förutsättningar', *Religion och Bibel, Nathan Söderblom-sällskapets Ärsbok*, VI, 1947, pp. 27-39

15 G. Dumézil, *op. cit*., p. 9:
'A la différence des l'Inde, les sociétés iraniennes n'ont pas durci cette conception en un régime de castes: elle semble être restée un modèle, un idéal, et aussi un moyen commode d'analyser et d'énoncer l'essentiel de la matière sociale.'

16 G. Dumézil, *ibid*, p. 10

17 G. Dumézil, *ibid*, p. 11: 'Les classes sociales chez les Celtes — Le cas le plus complet est celui des plus occidentaux des Indo-Européens, Celtes et Italiotes, — ce qui n'étonne pas, quand on a pris garde (J. Vendryes, 1918) aux nombreuses correspondances qui existent, dans le vocabulaire de la religion, de l'administration et du droit, entre les langues indo-iraniennes d'une part, les langues italiques et celtiques d'autre part, et elles seules.'

18 *Rig Veda* 21. 164, 46

19 Vedic times distinguish between three fires: the fire on earth, the fire in the air (lightning) and the fire in the sky (sun).
The triad of the Vedic gods related to the three fires and consisted of Agni, god of fire, Indra (or Vayu) god of war and thunder, and Surya (Mitra-Varuna), god of the sun.

20 Ralph Waldo Emerson, 'Nature 1836, Language, IV', *Selected Essays*

21 The dual nature of gods is illustrated in two of Lakshmi's other names: as Mahalakshmi (the great Lakshmi) she is also called Parvati and represents creative energy; under the name of Durga or Kali she is the warrior goddess. Thus the Great Goddess, symbolizing all creative and all destructive forces, becomes 'the mother whose laughter is heard over the cremation fields of the dead, eternally'.
(H. Zimmer, *Spiel um den Elefanten*, Köln, 1976, p. 174)

22 Early shamanic practices persisted in Indo-Tibetan Tantrism.
'Lamaism has preserved the Bon shamanic tradition almost in its entirety . . . Certain elements that contributed to the development of Lamaism are in all probability of Tantric, and perhaps Indian, origin.'
(M. Eliade, *Shamanism*, p. 434)

23 The caves north and south of the Tarim Basin were not only Buddhist
    centres. Nestorian Christians and Manichaeans also left a cultural
    impact. In the 10th century AD Moslem rule took over and Islam
    prevailed over the other religions.
    During the Buddhist period one can speak of an earlier, western,
    Tocharian period (Kucha and Kyzil) and of a later, eastern,
    Uiguric period (Turfan and Khocho). (E. Waldschmidt,
    Gandhara Kutscha Turfan, Leipzig, 1925, p. 34)

24 J.P. Mallory, *In Search of the Indo-Europeans*, p. 61. Tocharian
    speaking states of the Tarim Basin were Kucha, Karashahr and Turfan.
    The Tocharians spoke a type of Indo-European and the similarities
    shared between Tocharian, Celtic, Italic and Hittite were 'essentially
    archaic features inherited from the Proto-European language at a very
    early period . . . In the eastward expansion of Indo-European
    languages, Tocharian preceded Iranian into Turkestan and was later
    engulfed by Iranian-speaking Saka to the south, Sogdian and others
    to the west, and, if Iranian river names in the Minusinsk Basin are
    included, also to their northeast . . .' (J. P. Mallory, *ibid*, p. 61)
    'It is entirely possible that the ancestors of the Tocharians lurked
    behind some of those Andronovo variants that appear in the
    south-eastern area of its distribution. This would include
    Tadzhikistan and Kirghiziya to the west of the Tarim Basin where
    Andronovo related sites begin to appear by at least 1400 BC.'
    (J.P. Mallory, *ibid*, p. 62). See also Part I, note 26, of this Text.

25 M. Eliade, *op. cit.*, p. 440

26 A. von Le Coq, *Die Buddhistische Spätantike Mittelasiens*,
    Neue Bildwerke II, Berlin, 1933, fig. 163, p. 5: 'Man sieht einen
    Elefanten auf dem Rücken liegen und von einem Manne ausgeweidet
    werden.'

27 It would seem that the great individuality expressed in the late
    Luristan style resulted from the merging of two civilizations:
    that of the invading Kassites with the earlier Asian population of the
    Zagros mountains, the Elamites, whose civilization had once extended
    across southern Iran to the Indus Valley.

28 If we look towards the early Indus Valley Dravidian civilization of
    Mohenjo-daro and the seal of ca. 2300-1750 BC showing a seated 'yogi'
    figure surrounded by animals, we find the same refined features and
    the same spirituality. South Indian Shaiva cults had their roots in
    pre-Vedic Dravidian beliefs. Shiva, the yogi, was also the Master of
    Animals.

29 Since stylistic evidence seems to connect the Indus Valley Dravidian
    civilization with the style of later Luristan art — and therefore with
    Pictish art — we may also speculate whether non-Indo-European
    Dravidian words (which had appeared in Indic as early as the

Vedic period) could also have been retained in the Pictish vocabulary. 'Circumstantial evidence for identifying the language of the Indus Valley script with Elamite or Dravidian has been greatly strengthened by David McAlpin's work on the relationship between the Dravidian languages and Elamite.' (J.P. Mallory, *op. cit*., p. 44)

* * *

PART IV

Homelands

Chapter 1

The Hittites

A famous treaty between the kings of two peoples, the Hittites of Anatolia (Asia Minor) and the Mitanni of northern Syria, has provided historians with the earliest written evidence of the use of the Indo-Aryan language in areas north and north-west of the Euphrates. The treaty discovered in the archives of Boghazköy (the Hittite capital Hattusas) dates from about 1380 BC. The king of the Mitanni swears by the names of the native Hurrian gods, but he also invokes the names of the major Indian deities: Mitra, Varuna, Indra and the Nasatya. The treaty is thus concluded under the auspices of the sovereigns of the universe, Mitra and Varuna, who prevail over the order of the cosmos; under the powers of Indra, the god of war, also associated with the fires on earth and in heaven (the fires of the hearth, of the sun and of the lightning); under the goodwill of the twin gods Ashvin or Nasatya, who provide all earthly benefits.[1] G. Dumézil's ideology of the three functions is clearly discernible in this trilogy of heavenly powers.

Historians believe that a continuum of Indo-Iranian languages had begun to diverge from areas north of India by at least 2500 BC. Indo-Iranian people, speaking a language near to the future Indian Vedic, spread west to the Euphrates and as far as Palestine. Babylonian and Egyptian texts call these people the *marianni*, 'warrior bands'. From a branch of these Indic intruders the Mitanni kingdom in Hurrian lands emerged. Hurrian lands were non-Iranian territory where the original non-Indo-Aryan language continued to be used. With the collapse of the Mitanni kingdom by the end of the 14th century BC the presence of Indic elements in southwestern Asia begins to disappear.

The Hittites of Anatolia were also Bronze Age intruders who had assimilated an indigenous, non-Indo-European population. In contrast to the Mitanni, whose archives have not yet been discovered, the Hittites left us a vast collection of clay tablets spanning the period from 1650-1200 BC. In our research on the Picts the Hittites play a prominent rôle and we will therefore start with a short historical introduction.

The Indo-European Hittites made their first historical impact in Asia Minor by conquering the northern highland regions — defined by the river Halys (now Kizil Irmak) — which belonged to the indigenous people of Hatti. Exact dates and immigration routes are not known, but by 1600 BC the Hittites had expanded their domains southward and eastward. They conquered but did not hold Babylon, conquered and lost northern Syria several times and, after prolonged fights and skirmishes with the Indo-Iranian Mitanni of northern Mesopotamia, with Assyria and with Egypt, they finally established a firm hold on Syria in the 14th and 13th centuries BC and became one of the three great powers of Western Asia together with the kingdoms of Egypt and of Babylon.

Careful scholarly research has made it possible to read historical texts with almost complete certainty. We know most of the dates and names of kings beginning with the Old Kingdom established at Hattusas (Boghazköy) from 1680-1420 BC, followed by the Empire from 1420 to some time after 1205 BC. Thereafter Hittite records abruptly ceased and excavations testify to the complete destruction of the city of Hattusas by the 'People of the Sea', probably invaders from Thracia and the Aegean islands who joined forces with the northern Anatolian Kaska people. These sea-borne invaders attacked parts of Asia Minor's Aegean coast and, apart from overwhelming the Hittite lands of Hatti, also attacked Cilicia in the southern Taurus area, Cyprus and all of Syria, reaching the frontiers of Egypt.

Hittite culture survived for another 500 years in the Taurus area of modern Turkey and in Syria. It is thought that Cilician people from southern Anatolia probably joined the 'People of the Sea' and that some of them subsequently settled in Syria. The creation of the Neo-Hittite Kingdoms is attested by the Old Testament which calls the kings of Syrian principalities 'Kings of the Hittites'[2] and by Assyrian records which continued to refer to Syria and the Taurus area as the 'Land of Hatti'. The stone monuments of the Neo-Hittite Kingdoms bear long inscriptions in Hittite hieroglyphs but the language spoken was no longer the same as that of Hattusas.[3]

The Hittites made use of eight languages, with the addition of Hieroglyphic Hittite. The hieroglyphic inscriptions represented a south Anatolian Luwian dialect and scholars are now inclined to use the phrase 'Hieroglyphic Luwian'.

These languages consisted of local dialects and Hurrian (related to Armenian Urartu), Mitanni (an Aryan language akin to Sanskrit), Akkadian (Semitic) and Sumerian. The original non-Indo-European language of the indigenous Hatti people survived in priestly cults. All eight languages were found at the capital of Hattusas written in cuneiform on clay tablets.[4] Hieroglyphic Hittite was 'invented in the middle of the second millennium under the stimulus of increasing international contacts in the lands of the Levant, where the cultures of the Nile and the Euphrates met and mingled.' [5]

Chapter 2

Hittite Gods

Before the arrival of the Hittites the people of Anatolia already worshipped a weather god and a sun goddess, initially a mother goddess, and both deities remained predominant in the kingdom of the new rulers.

The functions of the Hittite weather god overlapped with those of a sun god, but the weather god remained supreme: a natural phenomenon when we consider the stormy weather conditions prevailing in Anatolian mountain regions. A very ancient cult of a god to whom the stag was sacred and who was 'a child of the open country' associated this god of the countryside with the *111* weather god as his servant and helper. A steatite relief from Yeniköy shows a god (whose name is concealed by an ideogram) standing on a stag, holding in his hand a hare and a falcon. The cult of the god of the stag was very widespread in Anatolia. The stag rarely counted as a sacred animal in the Near East, but it had been worshipped in the steppe lands of Central Asia and it is possible to see a continuity between the beliefs of the Eurasian steppe dwellers and those of the Hittites.

111 The god on the stag.
    A Hittite relief

Hittite gods belonged to groups of varied origins and were assimilated through a system of name substitution. The Hittite state religion adopted gods from the Indo-Iranian pantheon and by the 13th century BC the names of these gods are given in the Hurrian language. The Hurrian people were steeped in Babylonian traditions and transmitted Babylonian legends and the cult of the Mesopotamian gods to the Hittite ruling caste. Mesopotamian deities, such as Anu and Antu, Enlil and Ninlil, Ea and Damkina were introduced through the medium of Hurrian religion. Sanctuaries adhered to the main gods as well as to the many local deities. Hittite lands were known for their 'thousand gods and goddesses' and Hittite scribes attempted a syncretism treating similar deities as identical.

The Hittite weather god was called Teshub in the Hurrian language and Teshub's consort was called Hebat or Hepatu. She was a matronly figure and had initially no war-like character, although later linked to the Babylonian Ishtar who was also worshipped independently under the Hurrian name of Shaushka. As Shaushka she became the sister of the weather god and personified love as well as war. The same goddess, under another name, was the principal deity of the holy Hittite city of Arinna near Hattusas, where she was venerated as the sun goddess. The weather god, then her consort, took second place. At Hattusas, the Hittite capital, the sun goddess appeared as a winged figure standing on a lion. She was addressed as 'Queen of the Land of Hatti, Queen of Heaven and Earth, mistress of the kings and queens of the Land of Hatti, directing the government of the King and Queen of Hatti'.[6] The main weather god remained subordinate to her. The cult of Ishtar may also explain an ancient matrilineal system of succession and the independence of the later Hittite queens who could decide affairs of state, conduct independent correspondence and possessed their own official seal.

Hittite gods and heroes appear like ancestor figures to a Pictish inheritance. The mysterious 'dagger god' carved into a rock chamber at Yazilikaya is the 'Master of Animals', the master over cosmic forces, whose descendant on the cross-slab of **Meigle** no. 2 still imposes his will on wild beasts. The famous warrior god on the King's Gate of Hattusas (Boghazköy) holds a battle-axe which has lent its curvilinear design to many Pictish reliefs.

112

Pl 4
113

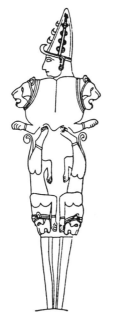

112 Dagger god, Yazilikaya   113 Warrior god, Boghazköy

Hittite figures betray a balanced simplification. A firm stance and a quiet nobility prevail and profiles show a spiritual refinement. The style of relief carving both at Yazilikaya as well as at Hattusas is of truly plastic form. At Yazilikaya the main gods wear the horned caps of divinity. They are supported by their animals which stand on mountain peaks. Beneath the feet of the main weather god mountain spirits wear the pointed hats of minor deities and support their master on their shoulders. At Alaja Hüyük orthostat reliefs are less plastic but the figures still impress by their strong outlines and engraved details. Hittite gods wear kilts with an oblique fold at the front. The king is shown with the long priestly gown and the round cap. He carries the *kalmus*, a curved shepherd's staff.

114   An Alaja Hüyük relief shows a king adoring a bull standing on a stele reminiscent of the Pictish stele. The bull bears the well known comma motif also known from Pictish images of bulls, boars and stags. Dot, comma and palmette signs also occur on stags of other
115   reliefs from the town wall of Alaja Hüyük, and in order to achieve a better understanding of the meaning of these and other mysterious signs linking people so far apart in time as the Hittites and the Picts we have to return once more to the studies of Georges Dumézil. All primitive art is religious art and any attempt at interpretation must therefore be guided by such thoughts in mind.

114   King adoring bull, at Alaja Hüyük

115   Deer, from town wall at Alaja Hüyük

Chapter 3

Pictish Symbolism in the Light of the Dumézilian Theory

71, 72   The Pictish discs with the 'Z-rod' image represent the symbol of cosmic principles: the sky and the earth linked by the spirit of creation (the Indic gods Mitra-Varuna) and crossed over by the spirit of war and destruction (the Indra-Vayu principle). In Part III of this book we have given a Mesopotamian interpretation to this diagram by mentioning the main deities Anu (the sky), Ki (the earth), linked by the supreme god Enlil, and crossed over by the god of storms and war Adad.

Dumézil has been able to prove that these same universal principles had been incorporated into the Indo-Aryan caste system which divided society into three main classes: kings and priests, warriors, and labourers. Included was also a fourth class, that of the conquered native people of pre-Aryan times, the *shudra*. Dumézil defines the Indo-Aryan hierarchic system by the principles represented by the *bráhman* — the linking of knowledge and mysticism; by the *kshatrá* — physical power and warlike forces; and by the *vish* — the grouping of people as peasants and labourers, also defined as 'organised settlements' (*habitat organisé*).[7]

The Indian Sanskrit word for the three (or four) social groups is *varna*, which implies the meaning 'colour'. The four Indian groups, *brahmanes*, *kshatriya*, *vaishya* and *shudra*, are often likened to the colours white, red, yellow and black. Indra, the god of war, and Agni, the god of fire, go through all three functions and the *Rig Veda* states of Agni that 'black, white, red is his way'.[8] White is attributed to the realm of the highest gods, red to the god of war and black or dark blue to the peasantry. The Indo-European Hittites practised the same symbolism: a Hittite *evocatio* urges the gods of a beleaguered town to leave it and come towards the victorious party on three different roads — the three gods to be dressed in a white robe, a red robe and a blue robe respectively.[9]

These basic colours — yellow, red and blue — are graphically incorporated in our modern 'additive' colour system where they form a *triquetra* sign with a white centre, created by overlapping

circles. Such colour symbolism was also known amongst the Celts
and the Romans, and it is precisely such a *triquetra* sign a Hittite
queen holds up in adoration in front of an altar.

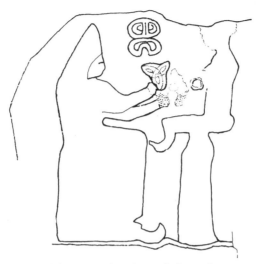

116   Queen Puduhepa holding up the sign of the *triquetra*
      in front of the altar of the sun goddess

The *triquetra* sign is clearly related
to the powers of the three main gods: the
powers of the sun, of the earth and of war.
In Pictland Queen Puduhepa's sign is not
only seen on the attacking lion of the front
panel of the Sarcophagus of **St. Andrews**
(Part II, chapter 1) but well known
examples of the *triquetra* are to be found:
on the back of the **Meigle** cross-slab no. 1;
on the cross-slab of **St. Vigeans** no. 7;
on a bronze brooch from **Glasgow**. The
basic *triquetra* signs evolved in Celtic and
Pictish art into numerous interlaced
motifs, as can be seen on the **Brodie stone**.

Pl. 1

Pl. 5

178

117

'piece

117 Triquetra sign on bronze brooch,
     Glasgow

116   The Hittite Queen Puduhepa was called the 'priestess of Arinna' and she is seen presenting the *triquetra* sign to the goddess of the sun, Hebat, (Mesopotamian Ishtar) who had her main sanctuary at Arinna. The goddess who takes part in all three functions, as the goddess of the sun, of war and of fertility, is also related in Indian mythology to the principle of speech and original truth. Speech and the utterance of truth form part of the highest, the priestly functions. As the Indian goddess of speech, Vac, she states quite bluntly in the *Rig Veda*: 'It is I who upholds both Mitra and Varuna, I who upholds Indra-Agni, I who upholds the two Ashvin'.[10]

118   A Hittite seal shows the goddess sitting on a garland. She is facing the weather god Teshub, who is standing on mountain tops. Another god, probably the sun god, standing on Varuna's *makara* with an antelope's head, is raising his hand in adoration. Behind this god we see the twin gods of the earth, the Ashvin or the Nasatya, standing on the sign of water. The goddess is accompanied by the rosette (the Venus star) and by the animals who relate to the three functions: the eagle of the sun, the lion who represents her warring capacity, and the bull, a fertility symbol in Hittite lands also related to the weather god. Bulls' horns appear as a particular distinction of supremacy in the crowns of Mesopotamian and Hittite gods.

118 A Hittite seal representing the Great Goddess

It is also possible to relate the tripartite ideology to certain signs on the haunches and bodies of horses, lions, bulls, stags and occasionally of goats seen on Assyrian and Hittite reliefs, on *9* Urartian, Luristan and Ziwiyeh bronzes, on Scythian metal work, on finds from the Oxus treasure and embroidered woollen cloths *11* from southern Siberia. These so-called dots, commas and half-*119* horseshoe motifs have always been explained as conventional devices to outline the principal muscles and ribs. In connection with Hittite art, Henri Frankfort, analyzing these designs, came to the conclusion that on the animals they 'seem additions rather than renderings of their anatomy'.[11] These curving shapes, and the dots, are symbols of fertility (see page 156).

119 Lion with human face,
and wings (sphinx). From Urartu

, 41, 43

Pl. 1

60

Incised on Luristan and Ziwiyeh lions we find Ishtar's rosette. Amongst the Picts we have traced the sign of the rosette in connection with the lion on the front panel of the Sarcophagus of **St. Andrews** (Part II, chapter 1), and on the headdress of the lady of the **Hilton of Cadboll** stone (Part II, chapter 5).

120 Lion from Urartu

121 Lion from Kayalidere

119, 120

122a

Incised on Assyrian, Iranian and Anatolian lions we also find mysterious 'tulip' shapes. On Urartian bronzes these shapes end in buds or knobs which show great similarity to the image of dagger hilts on Hittite seals. The 'tulip' shape is moreover so near to the Mesopotamian double lightning symbol that a linking of the two signs may be attempted. The weather god's dagger, the Hittite *li*, is associated with the double lightning fork on some Hittite seals. *60* A similar shape may also be detected on the **Hilton of Cadboll** stone, and we have already linked this sign with the weather god *122b, c* (Part II, chapter 5). Hittite hieroglyphic writing uses this 'tulip' shape, this time a stylization of the three-pronged lightning symbol, to designate the name of the weather god.

122a Babylonian double lightning fork symbol

122b Hittite symbol for weather god of Hatti

122c Hittite symbol for weather god of the sky

Also incised on Iranian and Scythian bronzes we see enigmatic *9* shapes like the letters N or M. These cryptic lines are also to be *119, 123* found on the haunches of horses and lions on Nimrud reliefs ('Assurnasirpal II at war' and 'Assurnasirpal II killing lions', British Museum). Such a shape can also be seen on the body of *124* a beast on the Pictish stone of **Meigle** no. 26, a relief which has stylistic similarities with the Guzana (Tell Halaf) animals depicted on a frieze of 'animal musicians'. (See chapter 5).

123 Little lion on gold pectoral from Ziwiyeh

124 Confronted beasts
Meigle no. 26 slab

Such signs are very like the Assyrian designs of 'fire' as seen on the relief from Kuyunjik, Nineveh, ('The sack of the city of Hamanu'). From Guzana comes the relief of bull-men supporting a winged sun-disc, a theme inspired by Assyrian and Hittite art. Incised on the thighs of the bull-men are flame-like designs identical to those on the Guzana relief of a striding lion. Similar flame-like designs appear on sphinxes and bulls on ivory reliefs found at Nimrud and Hama.

125

26, 127

125 Bull-men supporting
winged sun-disc, Guzana

126 Striding lion, Guzana

127 Sphinxes on ivory box from Nimrud

Seen in a Dumézilian light such fire symbols may be read as relating to the Indra-Agni combination, the war and fire gods inherent in all three functions. Once we have accepted the theory that animals are the protagonists of ideological functions and may represent the tripartite division so fundamental to life on earth we can no longer dismiss graphic signs on animal images as mere decorations or stylized muscle designs. If our deductions are correct in tracing the first two functions — the sun and the sky — in Ishtar's rosette, and war and fire in the lightning and flame symbols, then we must also hold the key to decipher the pictogram of the third function, that of fertility. It is a very obvious conclusion that the curving shapes seen on Pictish and Hittite stags, bulls and horses are in fact phallic symbols. The Picts also showed these symbols on wolves and wild boar. The Hittites combined phallic motifs on stags with a tripartite design, well known in the western world as the trilobal 'palmette' on the forehead of a Celtic god.

128, 129
130, 132

115
131

128 Pictish animals:

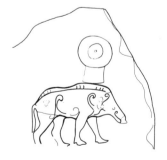

Bull from **Burghead**   Wolf from **Ardross**   Boar from **Knocknagael**

129 Stag on **Eassie** cross-slab

130 Stag hunt, Malatya

131 Head of Celtic deity, with palmette

Amongst the Pictish examples the most striking are several small slabs with bull images bearing such phallic symbols. The slabs are said to have been found in the well at **Burghead** where they may have been deposited as a votive offering. The style of the Burghead bulls comes very close to that of the late Hittite bull on a relief from near Ankara.

128

132

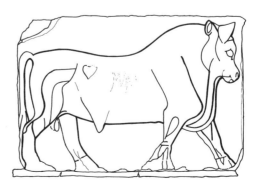

132 Late Hittite bull, from Ankara

157

133 It is also possible to interpret curved objects decorating the side of Hittite altars or gods' thrones as bulls' phallic symbols. We know that in the Indo-Iranian world 'ritual marriage' ceremonies took place on altars, ceremonies which must have related to fertility rites re-enacted to safeguard the prosperity of the tribe, the crops and the cattle.

133 Seated weather god with
adorant, Alaja Hüyük

134 A very crudely executed Pictish design, unfinished perhaps, on the symbol stone of **Gurness** may be read as the depiction of three altars. The altar to the left is topped by faint signs of fire, the middle altar bears the symbol of the sun, while the altar to the right shows phallic symbols.

134 Symbol stone from **Gurness** (Orkney)

184 The Pictish diagram of a rectangle with 'comma'- like shapes protruding from two sides, **Cnoc-an-Fruich, Grantown,** Morayshire, may thus be the sketch of an altar with phallic symbols. It is so far only conjecture, which nevertheless may be open to interesting parallels of thought when we consider that the Hittite hieroglyphic sign for 'earth', two horizontal rectangles placed one above the other, comes very near to the Pictish diagram with the stag.

135 A phallic design may also be detected on the bull which is about to be ritually killed, on the damaged cross-slab of **St. Vigeans** no.7.

136 J. Anderson gives us a sketch of the scene on the back of the **Kirriemuir** cross-slab, where we see a stele or an altar decorated by a phallic image. A similar curved shape hanging down from a stele showing the symbol of the sun can just be detected on the restored

183 stone of the three warriors from the **Brough of Birsay**.

135 Sacrifice of a bull,
   St. Vigeans stone no. 7

136 Back of cross-slab
   Kirriemuir

Chapter 4

The Recurring Theme of the Bull

The bull has always been a symbol of strength and fertility. In pre-Vedic times the bull was the master of dance and music, an ecstatic expression of the forces of virility, happiness and creation. In Eastern thinking he stood for the transition between heaven and earth and male and female elements. Indian cosmology gave the white bull to the god of creation as well as to the god's female counterpart, the Great Goddess (in Hindu mythology the great Devi, also called the goddess Parvati or Mahalakshmi). The bull may thus also represent female energy and female creative forces. In prehistoric cave paintings of the Upper Paleolithic, from a period of about 25,000 to 10,000 BC, bovine animals (the bison and the aurochs) connect with female symbols — while the horse seems to be related to male phallic symbolism — according to one of the underlying themes of A. Leroi-Gourhan's studies of prehistoric art.[12] Could the Bull of Heaven given to the goddess Ishtar by the father of the gods in the Gilgamesh epic be a relict of prehistoric mythology?

Hinduism connected the veneration of the bull with high principles: his four legs symbolized 'truth, purity, compassion and generosity', and the very marks of his hooves were taken as a sign of luck. The black bull was given over to the god of death and the idea of destruction. Adad, the Mesopotamian tempest god, who could destroy the land, but also bring beneficent wind and welcome rain, is usually presented standing on a bull.

It has been pointed out that the strange shapes adorning the statue of the goddess Artemis of the town of Ephesos (founded in the 10th century BC on the western coast of Asia Minor as an Ionian colony) are in fact bulls' testicles. Similar shapes in gold were worn as earrings by a Sumerian princess at about 2600 BC.[13] As a symbol of fertility the bull was also considered to be the most valuable sacrifice which could be made to the gods of earth.[14]

Already in pre-historic Mesopotamia (the Halaf culture of northern Mesopotamia, ca. 5500-5000 BC) horns of cattle assume great importance. Akkadian gods later wear horns as a symbol of their status, and the semi-divine position of the Akkadian rulers is symbolized by the horns worn in their headgear. High Hittite gods followed this custom while lesser gods, such as the mountain spirits, have horns decorating their skirts.

The transition beween heaven and earth in the shape of the bull may even be traced as far as Korea, where curved jewels in jade and in beryl probably represented small horn ends; they were combined with metal sun discs and set into the royal crowns of the Three Kingdoms period, presumably as fertility symbols.

The magical potency of horns, antlers and tusks has always been with mankind. According to 'early manifestations of belief . . . the head contained the procreative element, a source of fertilizing liquid, and horns were a concentration of the life substance or psyche. Ideas like this were common to Scandinavia, Iran, Greece, Palestine, and Celtic lands. From them there stem the altar horns of Israel and Crete, the gilding of the horns of the sacrificial ox, the Iranian belief in an ox's horn as the tree of life, and the horned tiaras and helmets of gods and warriors wherever they occur'.[15]

Indian mythology even saw in the tail of a bull spiritual qualities: the touching of a bull's tail could be akin to spiritual cleansing. Understood in this context we cannot be sure whether Hittite hairstyles which assigned long 'tails' to warrior images did not have religious significance and whether such customs could not have prevailed amongst the Picts. The warrior god on the King's Gate of Hattusas wears his hair in a long plait. A Pictish relief on the **Inchbrayock** slab shows a man wearing a similar hairstyle.[16] He is approaching a goddess, his arm raised angularly in a gesture of adoration. The upward pointing shoes of the divine figure were originally worn in Anatolia by men and by gods, but by 700 BC this fashion was exclusively reserved for godly images.

113
137

137 Goddess with adorant, **Inchbrayock** slab

138 The Pictish divinity has a strong resemblance to the goddess of the basalt statue of Guzana (Tell Halaf), in the heart of the ancient Mitanni kingdom.[17] The Pictish illustration is crude and simplified, but both goddesses bear the same physionomy, they have the same gaunt look and broad smile, 'and the continuous curve from the tip of the nose, over the skull, to the ends of the hair hanging down the back'.[18]

138 Goddess from Guzana

Chapter 5

North Syrian Lands

The most striking stylistic evidence leading to a convincing conclusion on Pictish lands of origin reaches us, not from central Anatolia, but from south-eastern Anatolia and from northern Syria. Both areas had long been disputed by the Hittites and the Mitanni. In the 15th and 14th centuries BC Mitanni Hurrian kingdoms stretched from the area of lake Van in the north to Assur and Aleppo (Halab) in the south. By the 14th and 13th centuries northern Syria came under Hittite control and remained under Hittite cultural influence long after the Hittite empire had collapsed in 1200 BC.

After the fall of the Mitanni dynasty in the 13th century BC the Hurrians founded the kingdom of Urartu near lake Van, which became a great bronze working centre and which flourished from the 9th to the 6th centuries BC. Assyrian influences assimilated at Urartu eventually travelled north to Scythian lands (Kelermes), imbued south-eastern Anatolian towns and reached south as far as Palestine. Ishtar's star is seen on a lion from Beisan (Bet Sh'an, Israel) and the Assyrian 'tulip' shape — known from Nimrud and Nineveh reliefs — is seen on a bull from Byblos (Lebanon).[19]

The 'Sea Peoples' who had overrun most of Anatolia and the Hittite empire around 1200 BC started a wave of migrations. The actual events during the following centuries remain obscure and from 1200 to 900 BC we are faced with the dark ages of Greece, Asia Minor and the Levant.

During the 9th to the 6th centuries BC the bronze working centres of Urartu, Ziwiyeh, Hassanlu and Luristan developed their own art based on Sumerian, Assyrian, Scythian and Hittite influences. Bronzes from these centres therefore showed similarities of style and origins. It was in the heart of Mitanni country, at Guzana (Tell Halaf), and further west at Carchemish, towns belonging to northern Syria, that all these influences came together and continued to be developed.

Soon after 1000 BC Aramaean tribes from the desert penetrated into Syria and southern Mesopotamia. They spoke a language akin to Hebrew and Phoenician. The Assyrians, to whom north Syria had been part of the Hittite empire, were to include the Aramaeans amongst the 'Hittites' who inhabited 'the land of Hatti'. Northern Syria was subsequently ruled by princelings of Hittite, Syrian and Aramaean extraction who based their courtly life on Assyrian traditions. The prosperity and ultimate ruin (at the end of the 8th century BC when independent Syrian rulers were replaced by Assyrian military governors) of the various cities depended on their relations with Assyria.

Diverse foreign stimuli reigned in north Syria. Hittite rites continued to be practised in some north Syrian towns. At Malatya, for instance, Hittite costume was still depicted on reliefs in the first millennium BC. A continuity of Hittite traditions existed side by side with Assyrian courtly art. Hittite influences were strong in Malatya and Carchemish, Aramaean influences in Marash and Karatepe, while Assyrian influences and the style of Urartu were felt all over north Syria. There was no single ethnic basis and the north Syrian style, thus subjected to various influences, has never been quite defined.

Pictish images show a strong affinity with the reliefs of traditional Hittite styles of Malatya and Carchemish (1050-850 BC) and with the later Assyrian-Aramaean influences (850-700 BC) also prevailing in Marash, Sakjegözü, Zinjirli (ancient Sam'al), Karatepe, and Tell Halaf (ancient Guzana), the most eastern of the north Syrian towns.

A relief from the southern gate of the citadel of Zinjirli shows the Hittite weather god Teshub holding up two discs. Teshub's cap is typical of Sam'al and Carchemish fashions and near to Pictish fashion as we know it from the cap set on a stele on the **Golspie** stone. The double discs held up by Teshub so clearly relate to the Pictish double discs that the Hittite god almost serves as a graphic explanation of Pictish symbolism. The two discs of heaven and earth are firmly linked by the god's mighty grasp, his fist reaching out like the symbolic powers of thunder and war we have come to associate with Indra, with the overlapping functions of the Indic Vayu-Varuna principles and with Mesopotamian Enlil and his son Adad.[20]

139

179

139   The weather god Teshub
      from Zinjirli (Sam'al)

140

Another double disc symbol is known to us from the Phoenician trading post of Dougga near the ancient site of Carthage on the African coast of Tunis. The Phoenicians who traded from the Syro-Palestinian coast had assimilated art motifs from Egyptian, Hittite, Greek, Aramaean and Mesopotamian sources, which were then combined into a style pleasing for trade both east and west, but which showed little or no understanding of underlying religious ideas and no concern for original meaning. The engraving on the Tunis slab depicts Ishtar, the Hebrew Ashtoreth, who became the Tanit of Carthage. Ishtar-Tanit is facing the double disc symbol with raised arms, the gesture of veneration. The symbol is surmounted by the weather god's spear.

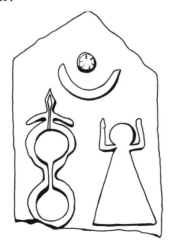

140   Ishtar-Tanit and double disc symbol, from Carthage

183   The three warriors of the symbol stone of **Brough of Birsay** (the tidal island off the north-west tip of Orkney) wear long robes and carry spears and rectangular shields. Such warriors in long garments also formed part of the Hittite army which fought against the Egyptians in 1275/4 BC at the battle of Kadesh on the *141, 142*   Orontes.[21] From the traditional Hittite style of Malatya and Carchemish comes the long fringed robe worn by kings, the hair-style with the curled up hair in the neck, the angular position of the arms and the stiffness of the figures. The same hairstyles survived in the Aramaean orientated world of Sakjegözü. The *139*   weather god from Zinjirli holding up the double disc symbol shows a profile and hairstyle similar to those of the Pictish chief.

141 King Katuwas, on relief from Carchemish

142   Goddess Kubaba,
      on relief fragment from Carchemish

The spiral motifs on the decorated shield of the Pictish king or leader are also typical for north Syrian art of late Hittite times, and may be seen on the base of the column at Tell Tayanat[22] and on a *143(a)* bracelet of an earlier date from the second city at Hissarlik, Troy, recovered by Schliemann.

143(a)   Bracelet from Hissarlik
         (Troy)

143(b)   Spiral patterns on metal
         belt from Boghazköy

143(b)   The fragment of a metal belt found at Boghazköy shows the same interlocked spiral pattern occurring frequently on Pictish Pl. 7   stones. The **Shandwick** stone and **Hilton of Cadboll** stone have *62*   similar interlaced designs — a pattern borrowed from the Aegean (the first period of Minoan art, ca. 1900-1600 BC) and repeated in Hittite as well as in Syrian designs of a later time. But we must not forget that 'Greece and her islands were settled first from the east

33

Pl. 6

178

144(a)
144(b)
145

146

and their arts were an extension of eastern styles, tempered by the peculiar quality with which the Aegean seems to touch everything that has its origin there'.[23] We are not far out if we call the twin spiral designs of fertility goddesses seen on stylized flowers on Cretan pottery (of about 1400 BC) 'plants from Ishtar's garden'. Indeed, the centaur on the back of the cross-slab at **Aberlemno** roadside carries a tree with its branches in the form of Ishtar's spiral symbols — according to the Gilgamesh epic, a tree from the forests of the Lebanon, where Ishtar was said to reside. Similar spiral fertility signs may also be seen on the cross-shaft of **St. Vigeans** no. 7. 'The sacredness of trees and plants, or rather the belief that divinity was manifest in the vegetable kingdom, was . . . one of the oldest tenets of Mesopotamian religion.'[24]

The kneeling Pictish archer on the back of the cross-slab of **St. Vigeans** no. 1 and the archer on the west face of the cross-slab of **Shandwick** have their ancestor on an ivory carving from Megiddo in Palestine, probably belonging to the 14th century BC. We also meet the kneeling bowman on an orthostat relief from the town wall of Alaja Hüyük of the 14-13th century BC, on Middle Assyrian seals ca. 1400-1200 BC, and on Syro-Hittite reliefs of the first millennium BC.[25]

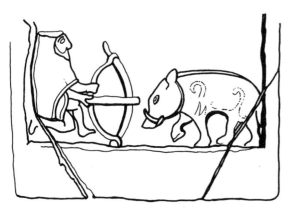

144(a) Archer hunting boar,
back of **St. Vigeans** no. 1 cross-slab

144(b) Archer hunting stag,
west face of **Shandwick** cross-slab

145 Archer on one side of
carved ivory rod, from Megiddo

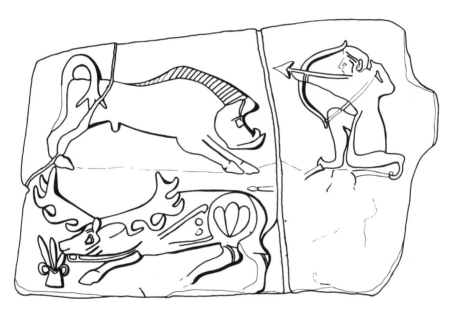

146 Archer hunting boar and stag
from town wall, Alaja Hüyük

55
Pl. 4

An Assyrian-Aramaean style from the 9th and 8th centuries BC is also seen in the central Gilgamesh theme of the **Meigle** no. 2 stone. The figure of the king reflects the Assyrianising style adapted by the north Syrian towns: the frontal stance, the restricted movement of the shoulders, the headdress and the trimmed beard are typical of the Assyrian manner. The three riders abreast on the left hand side above display a Sumerian and Assyrian way of dealing with perspective. We have only to look at the Nimrud reliefs of Assurnasirpal II to find a similar technique of silhouette - like outlines placed one behind the other to indicate a number of men or horses.

147   Top section of the back of the
cross-slab from **Aldbar**

Figures seated on high benches with footstools are common on Pictish reliefs, **Aldbar, Dunfallandy, Fowlis Wester, Kirriemuir**, St. **Vigeans** no. 7 illustrate this theme, and a comparison with a Carchemish relief of a goddess enthroned on the back of a lion becomes an almost obvious conclusion. The sturdy hooded figures on chairs of the **Dunfallandy** and **Kirriemuir** stones had their prototypes on grave steles from Marash. Seated figures from northern Syria have cube or oblong shapes and were also found at tomb chambers of Sam'al and Tell Halaf. It is equally a Tell Halaf characteristic to place orthostat scenes on narrow upright slabs.

147, 177
136, 178

148

149
150

148   Goddess Kubaba, enthroned on
the back of a lion, Carchemish

149 Lady and scribe
on grave stele, from Marash

150 Royal couple, from Guzana (Tell Halaf)

Very typical features of orthostats from north Syria and the
Levant (derived from Egypt) are the raised borders around the edge
of the stones — such as we see in Pictland on numerous examples:
the stones of **Meigle** nos. 2, 3, 4 and 5, **Eassie**, **Elgin**, **Hilton
of Cadboll**, **Dunfallandy**, **Aldbar** and **St. Vigeans** no. 1; on
the free-standing cross-shaft of **St. Andrews**, no. 19, the **Maiden
Stone**, the two cross-slabs of **Aberlemno**, and the **Brodie Stone**.

171

Pl. 8   The figures on the free-standing cross-slab of **St. Andrews** no. 19 are of a Karatepe type, a late Hittite-Aramaean style of about 700 BC. A general liveliness pervades the sculptures of Karatepe. The heavy profiles with prominent noses indicate strong Phoenician-Aramaean influences. A comparison of the **St. Andrews** cross-slab with an orthostat relief from the Karatepe

151   north portal, of mother and child, reveals the same primitive conception, the same floppy stance of the main figures, while the movements of the young boys flow out in dance-like gestures; a Phoenician influence has tinged the Karatepe style as well as the Karatepe theme of mother and suckling boy, which ultimately derived from Egypt. On the Pictish slab the naive style and puppet-like appearance of the figures is also continued in the animals of the lower panel. The scene with two birds and fabled animals could be set side by side with another Karatepe orthostat scene

152   showing birds attacking a prone deer or goat, and below this group, a hero with two rampant lions. The full-bodied sturdiness of these animals, like those on a frieze of an 'animal orchestra' at

124   Guzana,[26] is similar to that of the confronted beasts on **Meigle**
182   no. 26 and to the fantastic creatures on the **Murthly** slab.

151 Mother suckling child, Karatepe

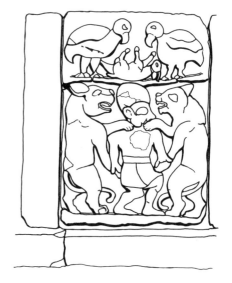

152 Hero with two lions and, above, two birds attacking a prone deer or goat, Karatepe

Pl. 8

153

54, 155

156

The plant branching out above the figures of the Pictish relief on **St. Andrews** no. 19 is no longer fully visible, but we can still detect a heavy primitive style, an Aramaean approach to the old Assyrian motif of the Tree of Life from 9th century BC Nimrud times. Touching the branch shown at the broken top of the Pictish stone are the hooves of a goat or an ibex. These animals, associated with the Tree of Life, are one of Ishtar's fertility symbols. The sacred tree is also known from Carchemish, Karatepe, Sakjegözü, Ziwiyeh and from a Mitannian seal. In fact the Indo-European Mitanni had originally introduced the image of the sacred tree into Mesopotamia.

153   Trees of Life on an embroidered tunic of Assurnasirpal, on a relief from Nimrud

154   Tree of Life, flanked by two goats, on a relief at Karetepe

155   Tree of Life on Mitanni seal impression

156   Tree of Life, flanked by two deities, on relief from Sakjegözü

A stylized tree held up by the Great Goddess and ending in buds of symbolic shapes (reminiscent of the three and two pronged lightning fork, the spear-head and antler shapes), is also known *157* from felt appliqué work of the 5th century BC from the remote area of Pazyryk in southern Siberia.

157 Tree of Life held by the Great Goddess.
Detail from a felt appliqué hanging
from Pazyryk

Pl. 6   The lower panel of the back of the cross-slab of **Aberlemno** shows a tree carried by a centaur, and the Pictish stylized tree is almost identical with the design of a sacred tree flanked by two *156* deities on a relief from Sakjegözü of the 8th century BC. A similarity to the Pictish theme of the centaur carrying a tree may *158* also be found in Phrygian architectural pottery plaques of about 600 BC from Pazarli (eastern Anatolia), where centaurs carry Pl. 4 realistic looking branches, like the one on **Meigle** no. 2.

158   Centaur carrying a tree,
on a pottery plaque,
from Pazarli

* * *

Following our examination of the stylistic evidence for Pictish origins in north Syrian lands, and bearing in mind Bede's statement that the Picts came to Scotland over Ireland, we ought to consider the Danunians. These people are 'now known to have lived round Adana in south-western Anatolia' (in fact in Luwian-speaking districts of Cilicia not far from ancient Karatepe) 'during the ninth to seventh centuries BC. They are probably related to Homer's Danaoi . . .'[27] The Danunians are mentioned by Ramses III among the 'Peoples of the Sea' whom he defeated around 1200 BC. They may also have called themselves the people of the goddess Inana (the Sumerian name for Ishtar) and a parallel with the Irish people of the goddess Danu or Anu, the Tuatha Dé Danann, makes an interesting comparison. The Irish Book of Invasions *Lebor Gabála Érenn* reports six invasions of Ireland, one of which was by the Tuatha Dé Danann, a tribe who were said to have come from 'the northern isles of the world, i.e. Greece.[28] The Tuatha Dé Danann brought four treasures with them to Ireland: a spear, a sword, a cauldron and a stone pillar, the Lia Fál, the place where the crowning of a king was sanctioned. According to Scottish tradition, however, the stone of Lia Fál was introduced into Ireland by the Dál Riada.[29] Twin hills known as the Paps near Killarney (Ireland) were called in Gaelic the 'breasts of Anu', the mythical mother of the last generation of gods that ruled the earth.[30] Although presented in the *Lebor Gabála* as a wave of invaders, the Tuatha Dé Danann appear in Irish myths as fairy people with magical powers.

The people of Adana may have been the survivors of migrations which took many inhabitants of south-west Anatolia into Syria during the 12th century BC. Could some of them have found their way to Ireland? And could their descendants have followed — with the consequences retold by Bede?

The Semitic languages spoken in Syria, such as Aramaic, might hold the key to the non-Indo-European element which existed in the Pictish language from pre-Celtic times down to the end of Pictish independence. In this connection we should also, consider the Hurrian language (which is probably related to the East Caucasian group of languages) spoken in eastern Anatolia. Hurrian was the major non-Indo-European language of northern Mesopotamia and the basic language used by the Mitanni (originally Indic-speaking people who formed a ruling dynasty over a native

Hurrian-speaking population). Among the Hurrian texts which have come down to us are also fragments of a translation of the Epic of Gilgamesh. A direct descendant of Hurrian is the later language of the kingdom of Urartu, called Vannic or Khaldian, dating from the seventh century BC. The Hurrian-Urartian language was eventually absorbed and disappeared as a linguistic entity through the intrusion of the Indo-European Armenians who occupied the Urartian kingdom around Lake Van. [31]

Concluding our survey of Pictish origins we may say that a north Syrian style of the ninth to the seventh centuries BC prevails in Pictish figurative art together with the nomadic inspired style of the metal working centres of Urartu, Ziwiyeh, Marlik, Hassanlu and Luristan. Pictish symbolism provides a clear visual link to Mesopotamian and also to Indo-Iranian Vedic beliefs. Furthermore, the Luristan style and the tribal totem of the Pictish elephant's skin established links to the pre-Vedic traditions of the Indus Valley civilization.

Bede's statement that the Picts came from Scythia may be more readily understood when we consider the intrusion of Scythian tribes during the seventh century BC into northern and southern Iranian areas, advancing as far as Syria. The Scythians helped the Medes and Babylonians to destroy Assyria. In the following century, after the Neo-Babylonian empire had been established and subsequently taken over by the Persians, the extraordinary *mélange* of races prevailing in the Mesopotamian peripheral areas was held together by the Persian dynasty of the Achaemenids under Cyrus II, the Great.[32] It stretched from the Indus to Cyprus, from Egyptian Memphis to Bactria, and from the Zagros areas to Armenia. Persian rule did not destroy the varied cultures of their vassal states but exploited and enhanced them. We do not know when the Pictish ancestors may originally have set out from these peripheral areas of Mesopotamia but that the Picts should have retained a style over so many centuries is quite in keeping with ancient history.

In Part V we will see how Christian influences were taken up by the Picts to complete the story of the unique synthesis of cultures which they achieved and preserved for posterity, expressively carved in stone.

Chapter 6

The Pictish Builder

To unravel the mysteries of old stones we had to consider ethnological, mythological, historical and art historical matters. Like roads from many directions these studies all led to the central point of enquiry and served to shed some light on Pictish origins. Archaic art and symbolism are always deeply rooted in religious feelings, indeed history and art history constantly interpret religious thought. Early religions and resulting philosophies thus may form a kind of synchronism with different sciences, which, although developing independently, can combine to illuminate a particular enquiry.

The builders of antiquity took recourse to yet another science neglected and almost lost to us in our present age: the science of geomancy, which originated in the East. Geomancy is the study of telluric and cosmic rays and their influence on life on Earth, a science which is now being revived in present-day geophysical and geobiological studies.

It is known that Greek and Roman settlements and towns were orientated according to atmospheric zones, and that their temples were built on a net of vertically and horizontally positioned 'lines of energy', referred to as 'the winds' by Greek builders.[33] Altars and godly images were placed at central points where such lines would cross in profusion at right angles and also diagonally. The knowledge of such polarized fields and lines is also still traceable in the outline and measurements of antique buildings in countries as far apart as Egypt, Crete, Malta, Nepal and Peru. Such measurements also seem to have been known to the Celts. Romanesque and Gothic churches in Europe partly continued this tradition and made use of particular powerful centres and zones to establish the holiness of a place.

Had the Pictish stones not mostly been removed from their original sites we would probably be able to include the Picts amongst the builders of antiquity who used these lines of energy. Polarized zones can be measured by radiesthetic methods, and the few Pictish stones still *in situ* seem to have been carefully positioned on dividing lines between positive and negative fields. The few stones we now consider to be still standing in their original position all reveal such dividing lines passing horizontally or vertically near their centre: *Clach Biorach*, the pointed stone of **Edderton**; the **Shandwick** stone; the **Strathpeffer** Eagle Stone; the **Cossans'** St. Orland's Stone; the **Picardy** Stone near Inch; the Craw Stone at **Rhynie** and the Maiden Stone near **Chapel of Garioch**. Moreover, since double disc symbols can contain spiral designs turning respectively in a negative or positive rotation, i.e., left or right, according to descending or ascending movements, and since cosmic rays 'descend' and telluric rays 'rise' we are once again led to the gods of old. In the symbolic double discs sky and earth are linked by the symbol of atmosphere and held in balance by a crossing line which, in geomantic terms, the Romans defined as the 'voice of Jupiter' himself.[34]

In the ruins of Pictish houses (at Gurness and Buckquoy on Orkney; Jarlshof, Shetland) we can still see a trefoil ground plan layout. The Gurness house became known as the 'Shamrock' because of this.[35] The trefoil symbol was known and used as a sacred sign in India (Harappan culture of Mohenjo-daro), in Mesopotamia and in Crete and Malta. The symbol occurs frequently on Celtic ornaments and on Pictish brooches,[36] and must have been of great religious significance to the Picts.

Spiral motifs on Pictish and Celtic works of art and monuments have always been interpreted as purely decorative, but this must have been secondary to their original meaning. Subtly set as scrolls into a background foliage (such as seen on the Pl. 1 Sarcophagus of **St. Andrews**), or as spiral ornaments built into the sign of the snake goddess (as seen on the panel of the **Shandwick** stone), as terminal ornaments incorporated with the symbol of the sacrificial axe (outlined within half-moon designs), they take on a deeper meaning. Indeed, the playful and decorative employment of such patterns belongs to an 'outer garment' of a deeply felt and realized archaic experience which, in religious and philosophical terms, takes on a universal significance. Earth, the material mother figure, and Heaven, our spiritual awareness, are linked, and the ultimate balance of life is symbolized by a line of energy crossing between the two astral bodies of Sun (Heaven) and Earth.

178

NOTES TO PART IV

1   The character of the sovereign gods Mitra and Varuna is expounded by
G. Dumézil as complementary elements in opposition establishing the
cosmic balance. G. Dumézil, *Les dieux souverains des Indo-Européens* ,
Paris,1977, p. 59: 'L'opposition de Mitra et de Varuna n'est jamais, ne
pouvait pas être hostilité ou rivalité, mais seulement complementarité.
Les deux dieux, avec les idées et les conduites qu'ils représentent,
sont également nécessaires à la vie des hommes et du cosmos. Ils ne se
rangent pas, quand ils sont opposés, l'un d'un côté 'bon', l'autre d'un
côté 'mauvais', même si quelques résonances ont été perçues dans ce
sens.'
The *Rig Veda* (1.115, 5) indicates the solar aspect of both gods;
Mitra represents the brilliant day-time sun, Varuna the dark
aspects of the night-time sun. See also Part V, chapter 4: *The Myth
of the Three Suns.*
The Indic twin gods Ashvin and Nasatya are always mentioned
collectively either as the Ashvin or the Nasatya.

2   2 *Kings* VII. 6;   2 *Chron.* I. 17

3   Approximate dating of Hittite history:

Hatti times:	2500-2000 BC
Early times:	2000-1680 BC
Old Kingdom:	1680-1420 BC
Empire:	1420-1200 BC
Neo-Hittite kingdoms:	1200-700 BC

4   The eight Hittite languages in cuneiform texts comprise:

1.   The original language of the land of Hatti. It survived in
priestly utterances in a number of cults and is probably related to
a group of languages spoken north of the Caucasus. It is not an
Indo-European language.

2.   The language of Hattili — now named Hittite — which should
strictly be called the language of Nesite or the Nesian language,
since it was first spoken in Nesa or Kanesh (Kültepe), the town
used by the Hittite conquerors before Hattusas became the capital
of the Old Kingdom. An Indo-European language.

3.   The Indo-European Luwian language from the western district of
Luwia or Arzawa.

4.   The Palaic language, also Indo-European which is attested only in the cult of one deity (Ziparwa).

5.   The Hurrian language used in numerous rituals. Fragments of the epic of Gilgamesh have been found in this language. It is thought to have originated east of the Caucasus. A direct descendant of Hurrian is Vannic or Khaldian spoken in the kingdom of Urartu near lake Van in the 7th century BC.

6.   The Indo-Aryan language which was used by the rulers of the Hurrian kingdom of Mitanni.

7.   The Akkadian language which was used in the Near East for diplomatic purposes. The Hittites knew this language as Babylonian and adopted it when dealing with southern and eastern neighbours. It is the name now given to the well known Semitic language of Babylon and Assyria.

8.   Sumerian, the oldest language of lower Mesopotamia. It died out at about 1800 BC and was thereafter only used by learned Hittite scribes.

5   O. R. Gurney, *The Hittites*, London, 1952, p. 105

6   O. R. Gurney, *ibid*, p. 115

7   G. Dumézil frequently points out that this system must not be taken too rigidly. In *L'idéologie tripartie des Indo-Européens* we read on page 8: 'Il est impossible de déterminer dans quelle mesure la pratique se conformait à cette structure théorique . . . L'hérédité, probable, à l'intérieur de chacune des classes, n'était-elle pas corrigée dans ses effets par un régime matrimonial plus souple et des possibilités de promotion? Malheureusement, seule la théorie nous est accessible.'

8   *Rig Veda* X, 20, 9.   G. Dumézil, *ibid*, p. 26

9   G. Dumézil, *ibid*, p. 26: an interpretation first given by V. Basanoff, *Keilschriftturk. aus Bogazköy*, VII, 60; J. Friedrich, *Der alte Orient*, XXV, 2, 1925, pp. 22-23

10   G. Dumézil, *op. cit.*, p. 36; RV X, 125 = AV, IV, 30

11   H. Frankfort, *The Art and Architecture of the Ancient Orient*, Penguin Books, London, 1954, p. 128; Yale University Press, 1970, p. 233

12   A. Leroi-Gourhan, *Les religions de la prehistoire, Paleolithique*, Presse Universitaire de France, Paris, 1964

13   J. Reade, *Mesopotamia*, London, 1991, p. 45: 'Pu-abi in the finery of death', a reconstruction based on evidence from her tomb at Ur.

14   G. Dumézil, (after L. Gerschel), *op. cit.*, p. 29

15   N. K. Sanders, *Prehistoric Art in Europe*, London, 1985, p. 70

16   I. Henderson, *The Picts*, London, 1967, ill. p. 147. The description
      by Isobel Henderson does however not tally with the opinion of
      the present writer.

17   The basalt statue of the goddess from the beginning of the first
      millennium BC had been built into the wall of the Guzana acropolis.
      It was removed to the Berlin Tell Halaf Museum, where it was
      destroyed during an air raid in 1943.

18   H. Frankfort, *op. cit.*, Penguin, p. 177; Yale, pp. 291-2; describing
      the 'primitive nature' of the Guzana sculpture.

19   H. Frankfort, *op. cit.*, granite stele of lions, Jerusalem Archaeological
      Museum: Penguin, plate 147; Yale, ill. 295; and ivory inlay from
      Byblos with image of bull, Louvre: Penguin, plate 149A; Yale, ill. 305

20   See note 16 in Part II

21   The battle of Kadesh which nearly annihilated the Egyptian forces
      under Ramses II was nevertheless represented as a great Egyptian
      victory on Egyptian reliefs, and we are fortunate to have detailed
      illustrations of the Hittite army.

22   The base of the column of Tell Tayanat is illustrated in H. Frankfort,
      op. cit., Penguin, plate 154B; Yale, ill. 336

23   J. Boardman, *Pre-Classical, From Crete to Archaic Greece*, London,
      1967, p. 15

24   H. Frankfort, *op. cit.*, Penguin, p. 68; Yale, p. 135

25   H. Frankfort, *ibid*, Penguin, p. 158; Yale, p. 269

26   The 'animal orchestra' frieze at Guzana, of early1st millennium BC,
      limestone 78 cm high, is illustrated in A. Parrot, *Nineveh and
      Babylon*, London, 1961, plate 100 on p. 91

27   H. Frankfort, *op. cit.*, Penguin, p. 164; Yale, p. 279

28   S. and P. F. Botheroyd, *Lexikon der Keltischen Mythologie*, Munich,
      1992, p. 335

29   S. and P. F. Botheroyd, *ibid*, p. 195. See also Part III, ch. 3, and the
      parallel with Scythian and Ossetian sagas.

30   Proinsias MacCana, 'Celtic Religion and Mythology,' *The Celts*,
      Venice, 1991, pp. 596-604

31   R. Ghirsman concluded that around 1800 BC there was a period of
      symbiosis of Indic and Hurrian elements in the Zagros. (*L'Iran et la
      Migration des Indo-Aryens et des Iraniens*, Leiden, 1977)
      See also Part III, note 29

32 Babylonian and biblical sources tell us that Cyrus practised the
    Babylonian and Assyrian cult of the god Marduk, the son of Ea.
    This cult should not be confused with the Sassanian Mazdaism.

33 M. L. Mettler, *Atmosphärische Reizstreifen, das Mass System
    antiker Völker*, Zürich, 1986, p. 11: reference to the writing of
    Hypodamus, a Greek architect of about 450 BC.

34 M. L. Mettler, *ibid*, p. 182

35 A. Ritchie, *Picts*, Edinburgh, 1989, p. 47

36 Moulds of brooches: A. Ritchie, *Brough of Birsay*, Edinburgh, 1986,
    p. 13
    Pictish brooches: S. Youngs (Ed.), *The Work of Angels*, London, 1989,
    ills. on pp. 94, 111, 113, 114, 116

* * *

PART V

The Impact of Christianity

Chapter 1

Pagan Symbolism and the Christian Cross
in the Caucasus

Syrian and Iranian styles, intermingled with nomadic Scythian and with Greek-Byzantine influences, appear again during the Christian era of the Transcaucasian and Caucasian countries of Armenia, Georgia (Iberia) and Caucasian Albania. During the first centuries AD a process of Christianization took place and, until the first impact of Arab invasions in the 7th century AD, the turbulent history of all three countries developed on parallel lines. Armenia assumed a leading rôle in accepting Christianity under St. Gregory, the Illuminator, in 301 AD, and Caucasian Albania and Georgia followed soon after. Many tribes, however, particularly in mountainous and secluded areas, were not prepared to go along with the new creed and the old pagan traditions lingered on and are still discernible in recent folk art.

Georgian stone reliefs and Armenian church façades display double or single ribbon motifs, garlands with runners and tendrils, creepers with lotuses and half or full palmettes, spiral motifs ending in lobes and circles, interspersed with realistic and fabled animals. Such themes, also traceable in Scythian art, formed part of an older Near Eastern repertoire dating back to the second millennium BC. It is no longer possible to trace the development of these pagan motifs which accompanied the Caucasian cross in Armenia, since all buildings prior to Christianity have been destroyed. Pagan motifs, however, persist well into the Christian Middle Ages and even beyond.

Pictish crosses have been likened to Armenian crosses.[1] Both appear on flat panels worked into reliefs and are set into highly decorated fields reminiscent of Eurasian and Iranian metal work. *159* Thus on a stele from Armenian Gaiana of the 9th to 10th century AD the cross is combined with images of confronted birds, trefoil designs and the Iranian rosette, once a manifestation of the goddess Ishtar. We are reminded that, already in early Sumerian art, combinations of herbivorous animals and plants always pointed to the Great Mother in her fertility aspect.[2]

159 Stele from church
at Gaiana

160   On many of the thousands of cross-slabs spread over Armenia
the last traces of the Indian *shrivatsa* sign of happiness may be
found in various forms. The goddess's wave-like and fish-like tails,
sometimes likened to a half-palmette, and shown in fine linear
interlace, support the crosses from the base. We have already been
22, 23   acquainted with this theme in Scythian and Celtic art. Identical
27 - 32 fish-tailed designs may also be seen on the stone reliefs of the door
posts of the great Indian stupa at Sanchi created during the first
century BC to the first century AD.

160 Stele from Etshmiadsin,
near Erewan

188

In Sumerian art and during the Old Babylonian and the Neo-Babylonian periods the divine emblem of mother and birth goddesses had the shape of the Greek *omega* sign (see p. 57), which was subsequently used in Christian times to identify Christ. The *Book of Revelation* 1:8 reads: 'I am Alpha and Omega, the beginning and the ending, saith the Lord . . .'

Herodotus mentions the Greek version of the origin of the Scythians.[3] They took their ancestry from Scythes, the son of a river goddess and of Herakles. The goddess was a 'viper-maiden— a creature which from the buttocks upwards was a woman, but below them a snake'. Ossetian sagas of the Caucasus still speak of the river goddess as their ancestral mother, a theme taken up in the many geometric and stylized designs accompanying the Armenian crosses.

At Ephesos, an Ionic colony founded in the 10th century BC on the west coast of Asia Minor, a great temple had once been erected, where the Great Goddess of fertility, the protectress of wild animals, the sun and moon goddess, was worshipped as the Ephesian Artemis. Later Ephesos was to become the capital of the Roman province of Asia, and Artemis became the Roman Diana. But where once Diana-Artemis had prevailed in the hearts of the people the Holy Virgin Mary was to find her place. We are reminded of St. Paul's mission in Roman Ephesus and of his denouncing the many silver statuettes of Artemis in favour of the new Christian religion. This resulted in a great meeting called by the town's silversmiths in the market place. We are told that this meeting culminated in an assembly of local people who shouted for two hours: 'Great is Artemis of the Ephesians!'[4]

It is again at Ephesus that, under the emperor Theodosius II, the Ecclesiastical Council of 431 declared the Virgin as the Magna Mater, the Mother who gave birth to God, and it is at Ephesus where the legendary grave of Mary is to be found. The transition from the pagan goddess to the Holy Mother was, however, fraught with difficulties. A late Latin inscription from a votive picture of Mary (in Baden Württemberg) quite humourously seems to sum up the tension between old and new beliefs: *Nisi fides prohibuisset deam esse credidissem* — 'if the Faith did not forbid it, I should have believed her to be a goddess'. On an unusual mural from Georgia another link with pagan times is clearly seen: the Saviour is shown between personifications of the sun and the moon, a theme which recalls Indo-Iranian mythology.[5]

The Urartian bronze-work style is still discernible on Armenian and Georgian reliefs, in the treatment of lions' manes for instance,[6] but the more realistic animal imagery predominating in Caucasian art takes its origin from Syria. The sturdy looks of the animals, the almost puppet-like voluminosity, are directly reminiscent of Syrian reliefs — and so is the setting. The vineyard scenes with animals and a king seated within a vine scroll, plucking grapes (such as seen on the façade of the church of the Holy Cross at Aght'amar, 915-921 AD) could have been inspired by north Syrian artists. A column capital of the church of Bagrat III at Kutais from the 12th century establishes the late familiarity with north Syrian art.[7]

161

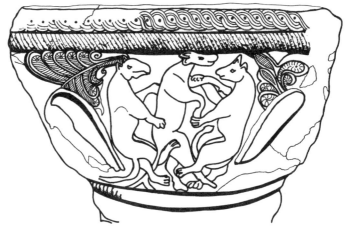

161 Column capital of the church of
Bagrat III at Kutais cathedral

On Pictish reliefs real or fabled animals in an Urartian and north Syrian manner occur so frequently that it is necessary to consider briefly Armenian history in order to understand how such styles could have reached the Caucasus and from there travelled north to Scotland.

* * *

After the collapse of the Hittite empire proto-Armenian tribes from south-east Europe, speaking an Indo-European language and who had settled in Phrygia, moved on to eastern Anatolia. There they eventually settled south-west of Urartu near Lake Van, an area later to be known as Armenia.[8] In the 6th century BC, under the influence first of the Medes and then of the Persians, these people formed a unity with the non-Indo-European speaking people of Urartu. Urartu lay north of Hurrian and Mitanni lands which had transmitted a highly developed Assyrian and Babylonian culture to the Hittites. Northern Mesopotamian and late Hittite influences had merged with Iranian nomadic culture. Towards the end of the 8th century BC invading Cimmerians had reached Asia Minor and the Zagros areas; they were followed by Scythian tribes, and by the 7th century BC bronze-working centres, such as Urartu in the north and Luristan in the south, had developed styles of their own, incorporating nomadic appreciation of ornament and decoration. In the following centuries Armenia, Syria and the Zagros areas continued to be linked by Persian expansion, trade and cultural exchanges.

Syrian influences must have been greatly encouraged during the first century BC when Armenia, under king Tigran, became one of the most powerful states of the Near East. By the year 70 BC Tigran's empire was vast and extended from the Caspian to the Mediterranean and from the Caucasus to Palestine and to Cilicia in southern Anatolia.

We can accept with a certain degree of historical authenticity that the process of christianizing Armenia could have started from Edessa in south-east Anatolia during the first century AD.[9] After 200 Edessa became a famous centre of Syrian-Christian teaching. Already before the time of St. Gregory two streams of christian-ization had existed in Armenia: the Greek type of Christianity and the Syrian type. Both traditions continued to survive side by side, and the Scriptures were read in the Greek as well as in the Syriac language. The creation of an Armenian alphabet by the end of the 4th century took both traditions into account and at the same time greatly contributed to the development of Armenian Christianity.[10] But Armenia remained torn between western— Byzantine and eastern — Persian rule. The Persians, who distrusted Greek-Byzantine influences, tried to establish their own religion of Mazdaism but eventually became aware of the impossibility of destroying the Christian creed. In opposing the Byzantine church they were forced to encourage Syriac tradition. Persian and Syriac styles survived side by side in Armenian church sculpture for many centuries.

Chapter 2

The Way North

The highly decorated style which had evolved around the Armenian crosses travelled to north German lands, and to the British Isles, along the old routes already established in Neolithic times between eastern central Europe and the Near East.

During the Early Bronze Age, trade in metal artefacts going north and amber from the Baltic areas exported south followed the close network of rivers which connected the Baltic with the Black Sea and the Caucasus, the Oder, the Vistula, the Neman and the Dvina, and overland routes connecting with the Dnieper and the Dniester. Other routes through central Europe branched off and crossed the Alps into northern Italy, or led further east to the Carpathians and south into Mycenaean Greece.[11]

Continental La Tène elements of the 4th century BC had appeared in Britain by the end of the 3rd century BC. By the first century BC Insular La Tène had achieved great refinement and an essentially British character. Roman conquest which had started in 43 AD did not tend to encourage Celtic identity. We have to wait for the major Saxon incursions early in the 5th century AD, which caused the Romans finally to withdraw from Britain, for a revival of La Tène art.

The Saxon sea raiders originally inhabited the north German plains between the Elbe and the Weser; the Angles lived in parts of southern Denmark. Both Angles and Saxons had absorbed La Tène influences and transmitted them to southern and subsequently northern Scandinavia. Thus these influences not only came to Britain with the Anglo-Saxon invasions in the 5th century AD[12] but also from north Denmark and southern Norway in the following century, and again, some 200 years later, during Viking times. We learn from Bede that the Northumbrians descended from the Angles who had come from the southern part of the Danish peninsula and from the Danish isles. The royal dynasty of East Anglia seems to have come from Sweden in the 6th century AD.

Very little is known about the Early Middle Ages. Their beginnings are set by some historians around the time of the Roman-Byzantine emperor Constantine the Great who, in 330 AD, had made Constantinople the capital of the eastern Roman empire and encouraged Christianity. The existence of a second Roman capital weakened the cohesion of the Roman empire. Menaced on all fronts the western empire finally collapsed in 476.[13] The early Middle Ages also mark the period of Great Migrations sparked off by the invasions from Central Asia of the Turkish-speaking Huns in the 4th to 5th centuries and of the Avars in the 6th to 7th centuries, which reached the borders of western Europe. The time from 400 to 600 in Europe, the Dark Ages, are 'lost ages' from an historian's point of view and research has to be guided by stylistic evidence.

* * *

Eastern influences in Anglo-Saxon and Northumbrian art are linked to a nature religion which incorporated animals and plants in close relationship, into a decorative design of patterns without end. The flat, worked over surface of Scythian metal work and of later Caucasian stone reliefs, so typical of Armenian and Georgian architectural ornaments and Armenian cross-slabs, was to have a strong influence on the North. Plant motifs, interwoven tendrils, 'inhabited vine scrolls' and abstracted patterns, extending over the whole visual field and terminated by ribbon ornaments, were taken over and no doubt also modified by a northern approach. But we may still see in Armenian and Pictish crosses and in Anglo-Saxon reliefs, as well as in northern ivory and metal work, a spirit more akin to eastern nature religion than to Mediterranean classicism.[14]

Celtic La Tène elements and later Christian Armenian elements may have travelled to the British Isles by various routes and at different times and taken up different influences on the way, but they converged in Scotland in the Northumbrian style of the Anglo-Saxons. To the Northumbrian inspired cross-slabs the Picts then added their own symbols and images, brought over from Mesopotamia, Luristan and north Syrian lands.

Another aspect of eastern influence in the North is found in the Scandinavian Vendel style, which has an abstracting tendency and consists mainly of swerved ribbon motifs ending in stylized heads of beasts.[15] The animal-headed horns or trumpets on the most interesting object which had found its way north, the *162* Gundestrup bowl,[16] come very near to the Vendel style.

162 Gundestrup bowl — inside panel showing sacrificial scene with a procession of warriors and musicians.

Although the Vendel style displays decorative motifs also found in late Roman art, its main features may be traced back to *13, 109* Luristan, where bronzes of beasts with elongated necks, oval heads *110* and beak-like mouths were being made at the beginning of the first millennium BC.[17]

The Vendel style is also found in Pictish art, where it stands in marked contrast to the Anglo-Saxon Northumbrian style. Northumbrian stone reliefs consisted of realistic fauna and flora set into meandering patterns, as may be seen on the front side *Pl. 1* panels of the **Sarcophagus of St. Andrews.** Close mesh interlace is also a Northumbrian style and we see it on the surviving side panels of the St. Andrews' Sarcophagus around realistically conceived scenes of twinned animals. The Scandinavian

194

Vendel style, which lasted from the 7th to the 9th centuries AD in Scandinavia, showed several stylistic phases but was always inclined towards abstraction. One of the side panels of **Sueno's Stone** (chapter 3) repeats a type of ornament current during the late Vendel period when stylized ribbons and loops were being displayed in a free and sophisticated way.

163   Silver objects in the Vendel style have been found on Pictish soil. The treasure hoard from **St. Ninian's Isle**, Shetland, contained silver bowls and chapes from sword scabbards which betray the Scandinavian style. Finds in Kent, Essex and Suffolk — the Sutton Hoo Treasure — indicate that metal work was being imported from Scandinavia.

The head decorating a gilt-bronze pin found at Golspie, Sutherland, and the portrait incised on a piece of slate from Jarlshof, Shetland, have both been described as Pictish heads.[18] But the head decorating the gilt-bronze pin is stylistically very near to the bronze head on a shaving blade found in a Danish grave and tentatively called by J. Brønstedt 'the oldest portrait of Denmark'.[19] The slate portrait has been described as the head of a Viking by O. Klindt-Jensen.[20]

163 One side of a silver chape from a sword scabbard.
St. Ninian's Isle hoard.

Chapter 3

The Norsemen

At about 800 AD the invasion of the Shetland Islands and the Orkneys took place from Norwegian Scandinavia. The Danes, the Norwegians and the Swedish people all belonged to the great group of Norsemen, the Vikings, who had set out to explore and colonize not only the northern coast of Scotland, but journeyed beyond to the Orkney and Shetland islands, the Faeroes, Iceland, Greenland and part of the east coast of North America, from Labrador as far south as the area around Boston. The Vikings also landed in northern Germany and in France, where we meet them again as the Normans. They invaded England and Ireland, settled on the Isle of Man, and travelled south following the French and Spanish coastline into the Mediterranean reaching the north Italian coast near Pisa. Viking presence in Russia was encouraged by two major trade routes. One led from the Baltic lake Ladoga along smaller rivers and overland connections to the upper Dnieper and then south into the Black Sea, and thence to Byzantium, Greece and the Palestinian coast. The other route, further east, followed the Volga to the Caspian Sea. When rapids had to be avoided, such as those found on the lower course of the Dnieper, the Vikings would carry their boats along the river bank. The Dnieper rapids were known by Nordic and by Slavonic names.

Connections with the East had been present in the north of Europe long before the Viking era. Already in 1200-1100 BC, during Early Bronze times, eastern type war axes, very similar in shape to those used by the Picts, were known in Scandinavia. Asian models of daggers and swords, and of the very individual curved-blade sword in particular, were being crudely imitated by Scandinavian craftsmen. Grave finds from Denmark and Sweden testify to the existence of small folding chairs made of wood with bronze parts, based on Mesopotamian and Cretan prototypes.

Sun symbols, probably linking up with an earlier megalithic sun culture, may have been re-introduced into Scandinavia during the Early Bronze Age.[21] The sun wagon of Trundholm, a large bronze sculpture of a horse set on wheels and drawing a gilded sphere behind it was found in a Danish bog. It leaves no doubt as to its once intended magical and protective purpose. Wheel designs on weapon hilts and on bronze ornaments such as dress pins testify to the veneration of the sacred disc. In southern Scandinavia sun symbols set on altars, not unlike the Pictish symbols, were carved on to rocks. The travelling sun could be drawn by a horse or by a stag; it could also be shown in a boat in the company of its animals or being held up by the phallic image of a man. It formed part of a nature cult together with the 'Tree of Life', dance and the sacrificial axe.[22]

The first Vikings who drew up their longboats on the shallow shores around northern Scotland were still heathens. They met with a Pictish population who had adopted certain aspects of Christianity under the missionaries St. Ninian and St. Columba.

'In the year of our Lord 565, when Justin the Younger succeeded Justinian and ruled as Emperor of Rome, a priest and abbot named Columba, distinguished by his monastic habit and life, came from Ireland to Britain to preach the word of God in the provinces of the northern Picts, which are separated from those of the southern Picts by a range of steep and desolate mountains. (The Grampians).

The southern Picts, who live on this side of the mountains, are said to have abandoned the errors of idolatry long before this date and accepted the true Faith through the preaching of Bishop Ninian, a most reverend and holy man of British race, who had been regularly instructed in the mysteries of the Christian Faith in Rome. Ninian's own episcopal see, named after Saint Martin and famous for its stately church, is now held by the English, and it is here that his body and those of many saints lie at rest. The place belongs to the province of Bernicia and is commonly known as *Candida Casa*, the White House, (Whithorn), because he built the church of stone, which was unusual among the Britons.

Columba arrived in Britain in the ninth year of the reign of the powerful Pictish king, Bride son of Meilochon; he converted that people to the Faith of Christ by his preaching and example, and received from them the island of Iona on which to found a monastery.'[23]

Norse cross-slabs show the transition from pagan myth to Christianity. The **Stone of Papil**, from the isle of Burra, Shetland, embodies the 'Tree of Life' into the Christian cross. *Papa* is the

98

old Norse word for priest or monk, and on either side of the short cross-shaft hooded figures of clerics are seen standing. Similar hooded figures with croziers also occur on the Stone of **Bressay**, Shetland. Squatting hooded figures are fitted into part of an arch from **Forteviot**, Perthshire. Three cloaked figures above two dragon or water monsters in typical Norse style are seen on the

185 reverse side of the **Invergowrie** cross-slab, Angus. These figures are not all necessarily clerics, as has been suggested, but probably Celtic gods, the *genii cucullati*, so called after the *cucullus*, a hood fastened to a cloak or coat. The *genii cucullati* appear in Britain in groups of three and were fertility spirits, and there is a possible link between them and monks, hermits, even pilgrims, who wear the heavy-weather coat of mountain people and ascetics.

The *genii cucullati*, sometimes displaying a phallus, stood for the renewal of life in Spring and the curative qualities of certain places or wells, a claim the Scriptures, which brought a new spiritual life to the people, could also make. Two of the Invergowrie figures also carry discs with engraved central crosses on their shoulders, and although we may explain these crosses as Christian symbols, we must be aware of the fact that such imagery had already occurred on Scandinavian rock pictures and amber amulets from the Early Bronze Age, as well as on Celtic bronze amulets. Its origins are even traceable back to pottery of around 3000 BC from the western Carpathian region.

Survival and renewal symbols may also be seen in martial combinations. Both the Papil and Bressay Stones make us aware of how near the arms of the crosses come to the old Pictish sign of the battle axe: a visual transition from the world of the fierce pagan warrior, who had to ensure the survival of his tribe through warfare, to the new Christian creed. A warlike combination is also

64 transmitted by the **Migvie** Stone already mentioned in connection

65 with the **Hilton of Cadboll** Stone (Part II, ch. 5). The incised pattern of the cross of the Migvie Stone is that of chain links combined with rings, which the Pictish artist has placed at the upper extremities and at the armpits of the cross. The image thus invokes the typical Celtic chain belt with attached rings to support the scabbard. We are also reminded of the importance of ritual binding to a god, an Indo-European conception. In the words of M. Eliade: '. . . the religious experiences induced by this same complex among the Hebrews prove that a very pure and profound religious life may find nourishment even in "bondage" to a God of terrible and "binding" appearance.' [24] The object on the left hand side of the shaft of the Migvie cross has a Danish counterpart in a flint dagger, a clumsy Scandinavian copy of an imported bronze weapon.[25] The style of the Migvie Stone is related to a stone in the Danish royal cemetery at Jelling in Jutland, where the image of Christ is incorporated into the chain design.[26] A Norse warlike approach is also to be found in the **Glenluce**, Wigtownshire, cross-slab where war axes are set into the chain design supporting a cross with arms of equal length. The Danish find of a mould (from Trend in north Jutland) with two crosses and Thor's hammer in the middle illustrates a silversmith's use of the symbols of two religions.[27]

178   The re-shaped cross-slab no. 7 at **St. Vigeans** has already been mentioned in connection with the *triquetra* sign (Part IV, ch. 3) and the ritual sacrifice of bulls (Part II, ch. 5). It contains the image of a man held upside down over a cauldron, which implies a sacrificial scene. An animal is also being held up on the right hand side of the stone. The sacrifice of men and animals which took place at the same time has been mentioned by Adam of Bremen, a chronist of the 11th century.[28] A similar scene of a man being sacrificed and held upside down by Teutates, the god of war,

162   himself, is shown on an inside panel of the silver Gundestrup bowl, a foreign import into Denmark. The bowl had been ritually damaged and then deposited on solid ground surrounded by a bog as an offering to a deity.[29]

Sueno's Stone in Forres (Moray) has always set a stylistic problem, since the figures are not of a typical Pictish style. The extremely weathered condition of the stone does not make any judgement easy, but the descriptive composition and the style of

164   the figures come near to the engraved picture stones of Gotland, Sweden, and to the figurative style seen on a stone cross from the Isle of Man and on the fragment of the Lindisfarne Stone from Holy Island, off the coast of Northumberland, from the time of the Viking invasions. The Gotland stones tell us stories we are no longer familiar with, although we are aware of shamanic influences, such as the importance of the smith and the man turned into a flying bird.

164 Detail of picture-stone from Tjängvide, Gotland

186   The scenes on **Sueno's Stone** have been related to battles fought in the mid-9th century between Pictish and Scottish forces and to the vanquishing of the Picts by the Scots under Kenneth MacAlpin. It has also been suggested that Sueno's Stone records the struggle between Picts and Norsemen during the late 9th or early 10th centuries. Yet another version relates the scenes on Sueno's Stone to royal dynastic strife, when the Scottish king Dubh was killed in 966 by his own kinsmen.[30]

    The decorative panels on the front on and around the cross-shaft are in an Anglian style, but the side panels of Sueno's Stone come close to a Norse late Vendel style (the panels on the right-hand side) and to the following Norse Jellinge style of ca. 900 to *165* 1000 AD (left-hand side panels). The Jellinge style received its name from a little silver cup from a royal grave at Jelling, Jutland, Denmark; it continued the ribbon-like ornaments and the elongated animal style known from Vendel times.

165 'Ribbon-animals' in the Jellinge style

The decorative scrolls incorporating plant and animal life and the pagan symbols of the war-axe and the dagger set around the Pictish Christian cross remind us once more of the Indo-Iranian triad illustrating the idea of fertility, of war and of spiritual salvation. Before Christianity had taken over, Scandinavian mythology had already known such a triad.

Nordic gods were part of a tripartite division. The functions of the godly dynasty of the *Vanir* were related to the riches of the earth and the waters; the *Vanir* were represented by father and son, Njörd and Frey (whose activities come near to those of the Ashvin-Nasatya twins), and by the goddess Freyja. The *Vanir* were the patrons of pleasure and fertility as well as of peace. The principal gods of another dynasty, that of the *Aesir*, were Thor and Odin. Thor was the god of brutal force, of thunder and of single combat. Odin was the great magician, the god of fury and of storms, the master of the runes, of speech and of the spiritual world, but also of war. The Scandinavian gods thus reflected the same ideological functions we already know from the Indo-Iranian and from the Pictish world before the advent of Christianity: those of a supreme god of ecstasy and wisdom strengthened by war and by the fertility of the land and of the people.[31]

Chapter 4

The 'Three Worlds' and the Christian God

The gods of the Indo-Iranian Universe belonged to their respective worlds of matters spiritual, matters of war, and matters of agricultural or nomadic life. To the Indo-European mind, the Universe was in a state of continuous change and the gods therefore also displayed overlapping functions. They were part of nature cycles of decline and ascent, where destruction and creation followed each other at regular intervals, and where the setting and rising sun and the seasons all embodied perpetual inflexions of life and death. Such conceptions of impermanence and transition, originally based on nomadic nature religion, were habitual to Indo-Iranian thinking. The central pole of a nomad's tent, the Tree of Life, or the mythical mountain, firmly rooted in the ground and yet stretching up into heaven, all symbolized the spirit of creation and the supporting axis around which opposites could interact.

The Indo-Iranian god of creation was the storm and thunder god whose lightning rod materialized into a spear. Often linked to mountains, he is also the mysterious sword god of Yazilikaya, and the Master of Animals who establishes a firm hold on opposing forces, creating the balance which maintains the Universe. Elements in opposition form an intergral part of Asian philosophies. They hide behind the mythical stories of human twins; they are indicated in the art of nomads when animals are arranged in pairs; and they occur in the theme of Luristan bronzes where the central god has assumed the shape of a human skeleton which symbolizes all aspects of creation: the pelvic cavity from which life was to grow, the rib-cage containing the 'wind' or the breath of life, and the head, the centre of all spiritual forces. All appearances are therefore interwoven and dependant on each other, and the gods transcend all Three Worlds.

The three divine worlds, of the Sun (magic and justice), of the Soil (fertility), and of victorious Combat, permeate Indo-Iranian myths. We are fortunate that recent research by Emilia Masson has

112
54, 109

shed new light on Hittite myths which have their correspondence in many Indo-European traditions. Three myths in particular bear a strong relationship to Pictish imagery.[32]

1. *The Myth of the Three Suns*

56, 89

Pictish stones occasionally show a third disc or astral body placed within a main circle, but off-centre, and therefore not quite seeming to form part of the main sphere. The pointed stone of **Edderton** (Easter Ross), Clach Biorach, and the stone of **Drimmies** provide us with such diagrams, and the key to their symbolism may well be found in eastern myths telling the story of the travelling sun.

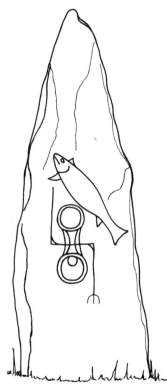

166 The pointed symbol stone of **Edderton**

We know from Mesopotamian myths that the sun god Shamash travels between heaven and earth and that the way of Shamash lay between the 'ways' of Enlil, the god of atmosphere, and Ea (Enki), the god of the subterranean fresh-water ocean. At the end of a day Shamash descends into a mountain to the west and, after a long journey underground during night on earth (caused by his disappearance from the sky), he rises again from another mountain to the east, marking the beginning of day. Akkadian seals show the sun god seated in a boat or, having risen from 'Ea's house of water', with fish caught in his hair. Masson tells us that Hittite inscriptions mention the Sun of the Sea or the Sun of the Waters,[33] for the Hittite god of the sun rises not from the mountains but from the sea; from the mythical waters of 'Ocean' the sun god ascends to heaven where he pronounces daily judgement over men, domesticated animals and wild beasts. In the *Rig Veda* a Vedic hymn to Savitr, god of the sun, describes his ancient path as 'well made in the middle realm of space', for 'Golden-handed Savitr moves busily between the two, between sky and earth'.[34]

The sun god thus lived in three domains, in heaven, on earth and underground, and the journey of the sun which detached itself from the sky created a third circle between the heavenly and earthly discs. Pictish mirror or gong images, which reflect the sun or repeat the chthonic sound of earth, are clearly constructed out of three discs. Such images are seen on the **Lindores** stone at Abdie (North-east Fife), on the stone from **Dunrobin**, on the **Aberlemno** stones, on the stone at **Glamis** Manse (Angus) and on the stone of **Meigle** no. 1. The Pictish mirror may thus be interpreted as a great symbol of transition reflecting all Three Worlds.

88, 87
Pl. 5

2. *The Myth of the Missing God*

Sumerian and Babylonian ritual myths recreated the descent of the goddess Ishtar into the Underworld. She went in search of her brother and lover Tammuz (Sumerian Dumuzi) who had been imprisoned in the Nether World. During the absence of Tammuz, who had been likened to Enlil in the older Sumerian version, the vegetation perished, and the absence of Ishtar herself caused all fertility on earth to fail. The myth of Tammuz was a fertility myth closely linked to the change of seasons, and the story may have arisen in former Sumerian mountainous homelands before the Sumerians settled by the Tigris-Euphrates delta. It was taken over by later people and used during seasonal rituals and New Year festivals. It was known to the Assyro-Babylonians, the Hittites, the Semites and the Celts.

The character of the Tammuz-Ishtar myth underwent several changes as it passed into different countries. The Hittite version of the story probably comes nearest to Celtic interpretation, since similar climatic conditions involving winter and spring seasons are found in Anatolian highlands and in European mountainous regions.

111

Tammuz has affinities with the Hittite god of pastures, Telepinus, who presided over the well-being of the people, the land and the animal world; he was shown standing on the back of a deer which, in the world of the nomads, symbolized the life of the tribe. Towards the end of the year he vanishes into the steppe or wilderness causing wintry conditions, drought and famine to set in. Earth and waters are frozen and the sun is hidden behind mists. All the gods then assemble and the sun god sends out his messenger, the eagle, to look for Telepinus, while the weather god batters at the gates of Telepinus' house, only to succeed in breaking his hammer. Telepinus has disappeared in a great rage and only another attack of fury will serve as the right catalyst to force about his return. This is achieved by the sting of a bee which,

57, 168

as the messenger of the Great Goddess, travels freely between the three worlds of the sky, the earth and the Underworld.[35]

167 Gold plaque of Bee Goddess from Rhodes

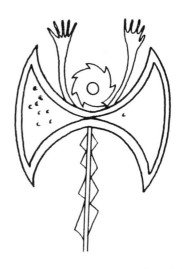

168 Painted representation of goddess with wings in the shape of a double axe on a floral stem. Crete

Telepinus, the son of the weather god, also personifies his father for, in Indo-Iranian religion, father and son could be one. The Hittite Tree of Life (our European maypole) associated with Telepinus, the 'God of the Countryside', is therefore hung with the magic fleece of a sheep or lamb, which contains all the good things of life; the tree is also hung with the quiver of a war lord.[36]

In Celtic mythology Telepinus is Cernunnos, the god with the antlers, who can also be shown with the legs of a deer. He is related to the god of thunder, Taranis, whose wife, the goddess Rigani, descends into the Underworld to free Cernunnos. Only through their union is life on earth possible. Cernunnos, once returned to the world in Springtime, is given the name of Esus. Esus is a fertility god linked to the Tree of Life and to the magic mistletoe plant, but he can also be a god of war, and the enormous complexities of overlapping godly functions are once more apparent in the Celtic Taranis-Rigani-Esus triad.

52 The Pictish Cernunnos seen on the slab of **Meigle** no. 22 wears serpentine coils instead of antlers and his crossed over legs have become entwined snakes ending in fishtails. He is truly a god of the dark earth and the animals on either side, a bear and a wolf, confirm his chthonic bonds. In Hittite myth the wolf is associated with the dark mists of a frozen and sterile countryside and his appearance strikes man with the same terror as chaos and deadly conditions of winter might do. Celtic iconography attributes to the wolf a protective as well as an aggressive character, and the same wide orbit of action is given to the bear, who represents physical strength, while the female bear is considered to be a model of motherhood and care. As the bear hibernates in a cave and then sets forth again in Spring he has also been associated with earth spirits and regenerative powers. The Pictish Cernunnos, flanked by a wolf and a bear, acts as a centre of balance to these cosmic energies.[37]

3. *The Combat of Creation*

According to Babylonian myth a snake dragon, Tiamat, lived in the salt-water Ocean and had to be destroyed before the world could be set in good order. Tiamat represented the original state of Chaos and only the monster's death could assure a situation of permanence and stability. During Hittite New Year festivals this myth was being re-enacted and the snake dragon Illuyankas, who represented the terrors of a barren earth, was then slain by the weather god. The same myth may be traced in India, when Varuna, the god who presided over Cosmic order and who was linked in Vedic times to the god of the sun — as well as Indra, the god of war — both defeated a snake dragon. The snake dragon has certain features in common with the *makara* who became the vehicle of Varuna.

169 The weather god fighting the snake dragon of Chaos. Malatya

169   A bas-relief from Hittite Malatya depicts the weather god Teshub, helped by another god, fighting the snake monster which is advancing under torrents of rain and hailstones. During the winter solstice the dragon of darkness is responsible for the disappearance of the sun, and the weather god's victory alone will set the sun free again to rise in the sky for 'mortal man to behold'.[38]

79, 170   On Pictish stones the nearest versions to the snake monster of Malatya are seen on the stones of **Golspie** and of **St. Vigeans** no. 1, where the monsters appear in pairs and not single; dragons in opposition emphasised good and evil qualities competing to rule the world.[39]

180

171

172

The back of the cross-slab of **Meigle** no. 4 displays a pattern of coiled-up vipers very similar to those on a steatite relief on the cover of a lamp from Neo-Sumerian times. That in India such coils of twinned snakes were also considered as knots of eternity may serve to illustrate how the Eastern mind accepted transition and contention, and how the animal world represented the worship of great natural forces.

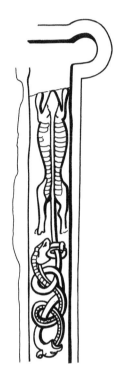

170   Pairs of snakes and snake-dragon
on back of **St. Vigeans** no. 1
cross-slab (detail)

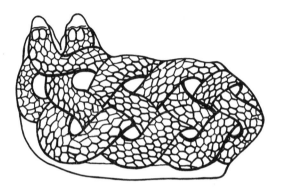

171   Steatite cover of lamp
with coiled snakes. Neo-Sumerian

172   Votive stones with
snake motifs. India

* * *

Christianity no longer allowed for metamorphoses, and the sacred significance attached to 'bestiality' in its non-derogative sense was no longer accepted. Elements in opposition were now not understood in their complementary sense, but served to distinguish 'good' from 'evil'.

The people of Israel who had settled in Canaan looked back to the Semitic nomad and semi-nomad traditions of the Aramaean Chaldeans of southern Babylonia (under the leadership of Abraham, the 'Hebrew', who came from Ur some time during the middle of the 18th century BC); to the traditions of a later branch of Aramaean people (under the leadership of Jacob, also called 'Israel'); and to the traditions of Semitic pastoral tribes who fled from Egyptian territory during the end of the 13th century BC. All these invading pastoral tribes eventually merged with the Semitic people already established in Canaan and took over their agricultural rituals and seasonal feasts. The cult of the Canaan god Baal, also called Hadad, god of atmosphere, clouds and tempest, relied on the veneration of natural phenomena and suggests Mesopotamian influence.[40] Under Hebrew influence the sanctuaries of Baal were given over to the cult of Yahweh. Canaan lay within the sphere of influence of early Sumerian, Akkadian and Egyptian civilizations, and the abundance of mythological material which we find in the Old Testament clearly grew out of Mesopotamian, Syrian and Egyptian soil. The ramifications of Mesopotamian myths, Hebrew writings, which also relied on earlier Canaan sources, and later priestly editing and re-writing after the Exile, which tended to historicize earlier versions by relating them symbolically to the deliverance of Israel from Egypt, are manifold. We will therefore content ourselves to recall a few basic myths recurring in the Old Testament, which had their roots in Mesopotamian traditions and were subsequently transformed to suit Hebrew beliefs:-

The Paradise myth; the garden of Eden has similarities with the Sumerian land of Dilmun, and Eve, fashioned out of Adam's rib, bears a curious resemblance to a Sumerian goddess (Ninti, the 'lady of life', or the 'lady of the rib') who 'heals' a rib of the earth god Enki.[41]

The myth of the Babylonian Adapa, the Hebrew Adam, who deprived himself of the gift of immortality, as Gilgamesh had done before him.

The myth of the Deluge, which existed in Sumerian and Babylonian versions and formed part of the Gilgamesh epic. The wise man, the guardian of the far shores, is the Sumerian Ziusudra, the Akkadian Utnapishtim, and the Hebrew Noah.

The Sumerian myth of the shepherd-god Dumuzi (Akkadian Tammuz) and the farmer-god Enkimdu, recalling the Hebrew story of Cain and Abel and the feud between settled peasants and pastoral nomads.

The Hebrew myth of Creation associated with the Babylonian New Year festival; in the Babylonian version this myth is linked to the god Marduk who slays the dragon Tiamat. The Hebrew god Yahweh smites the water dragon Leviathan, who is also called Lotan and is slain by Baal in a Canaanite version.

Myth fragments such as the origins of the Giants and astral myths imply cults taken over from the Ancient World. They recur in amended form in the New Testament and in apocalyptic literature.

As Hebrew mythology developed through the teachings of the prophets, myths and sagas were often modified and part of the stories suppressed as they did not always harmonize with the official *cultus*. After the Exile the crude spirit of early nature religion was attacked by men like Hosea and Isaiah, but the stories were nevertheless carried on into Christianity, and the great Christian Apocalypse of St. John once more gathers up all the images of ancient myth and ritual pattern.

Hebrew religion brought in a new type of cult: a covenant relationship between a god and a nation. Yahweh, as the god of a 'chosen people', represented a new reality. Myth as we had known it from Babylonian sources had had a magical quality. This magical potency was no longer asked for. The prophets of Israel transferred the magic functions of rituals to a new plane by bringing in a conception of morality hitherto unknown. The moral forces represented by Yahweh in Israel and later by the Christian God had no more need of magic rituals. A change of symbolism took place and the power and glory of one god only, now a moral being, was being magnified.

In the first book of Moses, *Genesis* I, we read:
'26. And God said, Let us make man in our image, after our likeness: and let them have dominion over the fish of the sea, and over

the fowl of the air, and over the cattle, and over all the earth, and over every creeping thing that creepeth upon the earth.

27. So God created man in his own image, in the image of God created he him; male and female created he them.

28. And God blessed them, and God said unto them, Be fruitful, and multiply, and replenish the earth, and subdue it; and have dominion over the fish of the sea, and over the fowl of the air, and over every living thing that moveth upon the earth.'

It was never in the spirit of archaic religion to 'have dominion' over nature. Supremacy over nature stems from a rationalized approach. Primitive man lived within natural laws to which even the gods were subjected. The Old Testament exemplified and affirmed the pre-eminence of man over nature and gave it religious sanction.

The biblical stories told by the Christian missionaries could not have been altogether new to the Picts. They included the same myths brought over from former Pictish homelands but now given a different meaning. Although Pictish art flourished under the Cross the Christian interpretation of the old Pictish beliefs must have undermined Pictish culture. The new creed which 'converted the wild beasts, that is to say the wicked man',[42] re-interpreted the character of the wild animals and saw in the motif of the chase the conversion of sinners, and was opposed to nature religion. The old Aryan gods became dark and malignant spirits and Pictish identity must have been suppressed by the Christian religion which had introduced the symbolism of a 'new creation'. The new Christian idea of redemption required an acceptance of suffering and complete surrender. The Christian assurance of salvation and the sacrifice of God's Son Himself on behalf of humanity established a new morality.

We cannot explain away the disappearance of the Picts in the 9th century AD by military defeat only, whether at the hands of the Dalriada under Kenneth MacAlpin or as a consequence of continuous struggle against the Dalriada Scots and the Britons of Strathclyde, the Angles of Northumbria and the Vikings. The Picts were truly conquered by a Christian God and it was inevitable that they should be assimilated and disappear from history.

The sagas of the Nart, the mythical ancestors of the Ossetes, foretold such an ending. Batrads, the last hero of the old Ossetian people, bears all the characteristics of a war-like Scythian storm and thunder god. His birth and death are connected with water; he rises out of the sea and perishes from an inner fire which he cannot control, since the element water is denied him by a mighty 'god of all gods'. After the death of Batrads the first Christian holy places rise out of the three tears which God has shed as a tribute to the dead hero.[43] The Nart proceed to challenge God who gives them a choice between complete defeat and partial survival. The proud answer of the Nart is, that should the end be inevitable they would not like to be known in history by a few weak survivors. Should the 'god of all gods' vanquish them, they would demand from him not a few descendants but eternal glory.

The rocks into which the Picts have inscribed their beliefs are still there and speak of the glory of a people so long forgotten and misunderstood. Reflected in the art of the Pictish people are the appreciation and veneration of natural laws, and a common cultural inheritance of East and West. The understanding and acceptance of such a bequest may have become fundamental to the survival of all of humanity.

NOTES TO PART V

1   J. Strzygowski, *Die Baukunst der Armenier und Europa*, Vienna,
    1918, Vols I and II, pp. 257, 719, 720

2   H. Frankfort, *The Art and Architecture of the Ancient Orient*,
    Penguin, p. 17; Yale, p. 37

3   Herodotus, *The Histories*, IV, 9-12

4   *The Acts of the Apostles*, XIX, 23-41

5   Fresco painting from the apse of the cave church of Dodo at David-
    Garedzha, 8th-9th century AD.

6   Lions from the capital of the south pilaster of the altar screen in
    the Sion at Bolinsk, Georgia, 5th century AD. (Photograph in Tamara
    Talbot Rice, *Ancient Arts of Central Asia*, ill. 222)

7   An interesting link to paganism is provided by 7th century
    depictions of king Tiridates III who had finally supported St. Gregory
    in introducing Christianity in Armenia. The king is shown wearing
    a boar's head, sometimes combined with a halo. To the Celts the
    wild boar was connected with Teutates, the god of war, and Celtic
    warrior helmets were often decorated with boar effigies. (See fig. 162,
    one of the inside panels of the Gundestrup bowl).

8   The origins of the Armenians remain obscure. Herodotus informs us
    that the Armenians were 'Phrygian colonists . . . armed in the
    Phrygian fashion'. (*The Histories*, VII, 73).
    'The proto-Armenians apparently rose to power in the Armenian
    mountains after the collapse of the Urartian state and were
    certainly present there in the last half of the first millennium BC.
    The Armenian language then absorbed a vast quantity of foreign
    vocabulary from its neighbours, especially Iranian and Aramaic,
    the Semitic language spoken in north Mesopotamia . . .' J. P. Mallory,
    In Search of the Indo-Europeans, p. 34

9   K. Sarkissian, *The Council of Chalcedon and the Armenian Church*,
    London, 1965, Chap. 3

10 The Armenian alphabet was created towards the end of the 4th
    century AD by St. Mesrop Mastoc, who later came to be known as
    the 'Father of Armenian literature'.

11 During the Early Bronze Age Near Eastern metal forms from sites
    in Syria, Palestine, Mesopotamia and Iran found their way to the
    north. The spiral motif was already known in metal work by
    2000 BC and 'there is no doubt' . . . that 'flanged and flat axes were

first made in the Near East'. M. Gimbutas, *Bronze Age Cultures in Central and Eastern Europe*, The Hague, 1965, p. 33

12   Bede, *Ecclesiastical History of the English People*, I, 15

13   The eastern Byzantine empire lasted until 1453 AD when the Turks conquered Constantinople.

14   It has been pointed out that the Armenian approach to decoration in architecture does not stem from Mediterranean influences but from eastern styles, which applied lavish decoration to finished buildings in a Persian manner. Mediterranean building tended to incorporate natural plant forms into the architectural structure itself. J. Strzygowski, *op. cit.*, Vol. I, pp. 451-2; and *Altai-Iran und Völkerwanderung*, Leipzig, 1917, pp. 150, 218. Strzygowski also was of the opinion that Indian cupola building and Iranian barrel-vaulted building provided the underlying principles of Armenian architecture, and that Armenian vaulted constructions subsequently influenced western architecture.
(*Die Baukunst der Armenier und Europa*, Vols I and II, pp. 341, 342, 711-14.)

15   The Vendel period takes its name from richly appointed boat graves excavated at Vendel in Uppland, central Sweden. The burials are evenly distributed over the period from 600-1050 AD. The Vendel style proper is however placed by art historians into the period from ca 600-800 AD.

16   The Gundestrup bowl is also mentioned in Part I, ch. 6, p.55 ; Part II, ch. 5, p.95 ; Part V, ch. 3, p. 199

17   The typical Luristan style reached its peak in the 8th and 7th centuries BC. An earlier style, more realistic, can be traced back to Sumerian and later Babylonian influences.

18   A. Ritchie, *Picts*, p. 5

19   J. Brønstedt, *Nordische Vorzeit*, Vol. II, Bronzezeit in Dänemark, p. 149

20   O. Klindt-Jensen, *The World of the Vikings*, New York, 1970, p. 41

21   This development was suggested by J. Brønstedt, *op. cit.*, p. 87

22   Rock pictures from Tanum, Bohuslän, Sweden.

23   Bede, *op. cit.*, III, 4. Translation by Leo Sherley-Price, revised by R. E. Latham.

24   M. Eliade, *Images and Symbols*, p. 124

25   J. Brønstedt, *op. cit.*, pp. 17-19; illustration of blade part of a dagger from Serup, Fünen.

26   O. Klindt-Jensen, *op. cit.*, pp. 128-9

27   J. Brønstedt, *op. cit.*, Vol. III, Eisenzeit in Dänemark, illustration on p. 380

28   Adam of Bremen, *Gesta Hammaburgensis ecclesiae pontificum*, ca 1075 AD.

29   See Part I, ch. 6 and note 39

30   A. Ritchie and D. J. Breeze, *Invaders of Scotland*, Edinburgh,1991, p. 52

31   G. Dumézil, *L'ideologie tripartie des Indo-Européens*, pp. 54-58,
      with reference to the studies of S. Wikander.
      G. Dumézil, *Les dieux souveraines des Indo-Européens,* Paris,1977,
      pp. 186-189: La triade des dieux d'Upsal.

32   E. Masson, *Le combat pour l'immortalité, Heritage indo-européen
      dans la mythologie anatolienne,* Paris, 1991: Les trois soleils;
      Renouveau de l'année agraire; La légende du combat avec le dragon.

33   E. Masson, *ibid* : Les trois soleils, p. 275

34   E. Masson, *ibid*, p. 275. The *Rig Veda*, 1. 35, 11, 9, after W. Doniger
      O'Flaherty, *The Rig Veda, an Anthology*, Penguin Classics, London,
      1981, pp. 198-9

35   E. Masson, *op. cit.* : Renouveau de l'année agraire, pp. 125-130. M.
      Gimbutas, *The Gods and Goddesses of Old Europe, 7000-3500 BC,*
      London, 1974, pp. 181-190, traces the image of the Great Goddess
      in the shape of a bee or an insect back to Neolithic times in Thessaly.
      Other representations of the 'Lady Bee' on gems and seals
      existed during the Minoan civilization. Minoan-Mycenaean art
      also depicted the Great Goddess in the shape of a butterfly,
      and one of the warlike attributes of the goddess, the double-axe,
      could also be used to represent butterfly wings. The image of the
      goddess as a butterfly continued to be engraved on double-axes
      during Minoan times.

36   E. Masson, *op. cit.* : Trois mondes, pp. 203-205; and Fig. 3, p. 140:
      Scènes gravées sur le rhyton de la collection N. Schimmel.

37   S. and P.F. Botheroyd, *op. cit.,* pp. 24, 28, 29

38   E. Masson, *op. cit.*: Vieux schème, p. 75, hymnes à Indra.
      A. P. Okladnikow, *op. cit.,* p. 62 and plate 18: in the Baikal
      area— outlined on the rocks of Shishkino — the mythical monster
      in the shape of a dragon is depicted about to swallow the sun.
      Ca 2000 BC.

39   E. Masson, *op. cit.* : Vieux schème, p. 77

40   *New Larousse Encyclopedia of Mythology*, London, 1968, p. 75:
      'Baal did not appear before the arrival of the Phoenicians on the
      Mediterranean coast when they emigrated from the Negeb, south
      of Palestine, where they had previously lived . . . But, as in all the
      other cases where a Canaanite divinity was called Ba'al, the name
      was never a proper name. It was an appellation that hid the god's
      true name, which was known only to the initiated.'

41   S. H. Hooke, *Middle Eastern Mythology*, London, 1963, 1991, p. 115:
      ' . . . the Sumerian word *ti* has the double meaning of "life" as well
      as "rib" . . . in the Hebrew myth the woman who was fashioned from
      Adam's rib was named by him Hawwah, meaning "Life" '.

42   J. Anderson, *Scotland in Early Christian Times*, Edinburgh, 1881,
      p. 167, from the *Hortus Deliciarum* or Garden of Delights, a
      manuscript of the 12th century which records Christian symbolism
      as taught by the early theologians.

43   G. Dumézil, *Légendes sur les Nartes*, Paris, 1930, pp. 69-73.
      There are several versions of the death of Batrads.
      The first holy places of the Christian Ossetians were:
      Tarandzelos, Mykalygabyrta, Rekom.

* * *

173 Front of cross-slab at Glamis Manse (Angus)

*174 Back of cross-slab at Cossans (Angus)
'St. Orland's Stone'*

220

175 Back of cross-slab in Aberlemno churchyard (Angus)

176 *Front of cross-slab, Dunfallandy.*
Near Pitlochry (Perth and Kinross)

222

177   *Back of cross-slab, Dunfallandy*

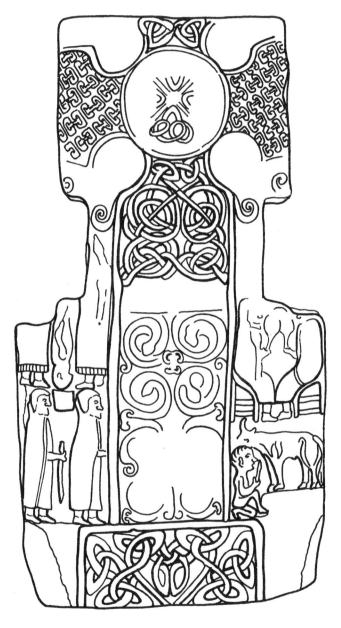

178 Front of cross-slab, St. Vigeans no. 7
St. Vigeans (Angus) Museum

179 Back of cross-slab from Golspie (Sutherland)
Dunrobin Castle Museum

180   Back of cross-slab, Meigle no. 4
Meigle Museum (Perth and Kinross)

*181 Front of cross-slab, Meigle no. 4
Meigle Museum*

*182 Front of slab from Murthly (Perth and Kinross)
Edinburgh, Royal Museum*

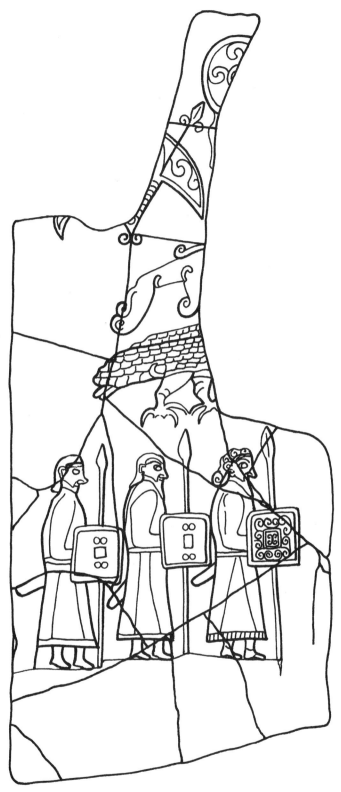

183   Fragments of front of slab from Brough of Birsay (Orkney)
Edinburgh, Royal Museum

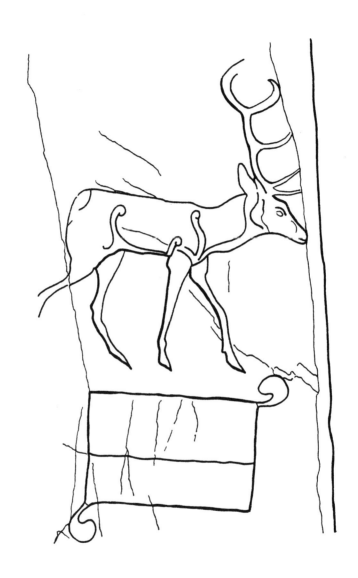

184   Stone from Cnoc-an-Fruich, Grantown (Moray)
Edinburgh, Royal Museum

185 Back of cross-slab from Invergowrie (Angus)
Edinburgh, Royal Museum

186   Back of cross-slab, Sueno's Stone, at Forres (Moray)

232

PLATE 1   The shrine or sarcophagus as displayed in Cathedral Museum
St. Andrews (Fife)

PLATE 2   The narrative front panel of the shrine or sarcophagus at St. Andrews

PLATE 3   Front of cross-slab, Meigle no. 2
Meigle Museum (Perth and Kinross)

PLATE 4   Back of cross-slab, Meigle no. 2

PLATE 5 Back of cross-slab, Meigle no. 1
Meigle Museum

PLATE 6 Back of cross-slab, Aberlemno
Aberlemno (Angus), at the roadside B 9134

PLATE 7   Back of Hilton of Cadboll stone
Edinburgh Royal Museum

PLATE 8   Shaft of free-standing cross, St. Andrews no. 19
St. Andrews, Cathedral Museum

PLATE 9   Front of cross-slab at Rossie Priory
(Perth and Kinross)

LIST OF THE PLATES

Photographs reproduced by kind permission of:

Cover: Historic Scotland, Edinburgh
Frontispiece: Edinburgh Central Library
Plates 1-6 and 8: Historic Scotland, Edinburgh
Plate 7: Royal Museum of Scotland, Edinburgh
Plate 9: Royal Commission on the Ancient and Historical
Monuments of Scotland, Edinburgh

LIST AND SOURCES OF ILLUSTRATIONS

All illustrations not otherwise attributed and all drawings
from photographs are by Frances Gilbert.

1 Part of a golden belt from Ziwiyeh. Late 7th century BC.
   Teheran, Archaeological Museum.
   (After photographs in A. Godard, *Le Trésor de Ziwiyé*,
   Haarlem,1950, fig. 48, p.57 and in E. Akurgal, *Urartäische
   und Altiranische Kunstzentren*, Ankara, 1968, fig. 103, p. 113)

2 Piece of a Celtic bronze mount on a wooden jug from
   Brno-Malomerice (Moravia). 3rd century BC. Brno,
   Moravské Museum.
   (After photographs in *The Celts*, Exhibition catalogue,
   Venice, 1991, covers and p. 376)

3 Typical Scythian horseman with drawn bow. A coin of
   the Scythian king Ateas (ATAIAS). 4th century BC.
   (After a photograph in R. Rolle, *Die Welt der Skythen* ,
   Frankfurt, 1980, p. 144)

4 Two Scythians with drinking horn. Golden relief ornament
   from a chieftain's headdress. 5cm high. Greco-Scythian.
   Second half of 4th century BC. From Kul-Oba kurgan,
   near Kerch, Crimea. St. Petersburg, Hermitage.
   (After a photograph in *Gold der Skythen* ,
   Exhibition catalogue, Munich, 1984, p. 123)

5 Scythian *kammenaja baba*. Stone 0.67m high.
   5th-4th century BC. From Ol'chovcik, Oblast'Doneck.
   (After a drawing in R. Rolle, op. cit., p. 36)

6 Panther in rolled animal style. Gold 9.3cm high.
   Scytho-Siberian. c. 600 BC. St. Petersburg, Hermitage,
   Peter I Siberian collection.
   (After a photograph in *Gold der Skythen* , p. 153)

7 Elk on a bird's claw. Part of a bronze ornament on harness.
   10.1cm high. Scythian animal style. First half of 5th
   century BC. From kurgan G, Zurovka, Kirovograd/Dnieper.
   St. Petersburg, Hermitage.
   (After a photograph in *Gold der Skythen* , p. 79)

8   Wolf and snake fighting. Gold ornamental plate of belt clasp.
    14.5cm wide. Scytho-Siberian. 4th century BC. St. Petersburg,
    Hermitage, Peter I Siberian collection.
    (After a photograph in *Gold der Skythen*, p. 162)

9   Two fabulous beasts from a procession of eight, in relief
    on a golden scabbard 47cm long. Near Eastern art with
    Scythian elements. End of 7th to early 6th century BC.
    From a kurgan in Kuban region (Krasnodar). St. Petersburg,
    Hermitage.
    (After a photograph in B. Piatrovski, L. Galanina and
    N. Grach, *Scythian Art*, Leningrad/Oxford, 1987, nos. 32-5)

10 Fabulous beast. Bronze part of horse bridle. 13.5cm long.
    Scythian. 4th century BC. From kurgan Elizavetinskaja
    Stanisa, Kuban region. St. Petersburg, Hermitage.
    (After a photograph in *Gold der Skythen*, p. 136)

11 Lion. Detail from a bronze shield of Sardur II. 760-730 BC.
    Old Urartian style.
    (E.Akurgal, *op. cit.*, fig. 20, p. 57)

12 Winged lion. Detail from a pectoral from Ziwiyeh.
    Second half of 7th century BC.
    (E. Akurgal, *op. cit.*, fig. 32, p. 64)

13 Twin elongated beasts. Bronze. Luristan. 7th century BC.
    Boston. Museum of Fine Arts.
    (E. Akurgal, *op. cit.*, fig. 36, p. 66 and back cover)

14 Snaffle with animal and bird heads. Wood. 18cm long.
    Scytho-Siberian animal style. Early 4th century BC.
    From kurgan 3, Pazyryk, Altai. St. Petersburg, Hermitage.
    (After a photograph in *Gold der Skythen*, p. 208)

15 Bronze mirror disc with two entwined animals. 6.2cm diam.
    Early nomadic culture. 5th-3rd centuries BC.
    From a kurgan near Tuva. St. Petersburg, Hermitage.
    (After a photograph in *Gold der Skythen*, p. 234)

16 Bronze torque with tigers. 17.5cm diam. Early nomadic
    culture. 5/4th century BC. From Siberia. St. Petersburg,
    Hermitage. (After a photograph in *Gold der Skythen*, p. 233)

17 Stag. Wood, with leather antlers and ears (originally covered
    with gold leaf). 11cm high. Scytho-Siberian animal style.
    Late 5th century BC. From kurgan Z, Pazyryk, Altai.
    St. Petersburg, Hermitage.
    (After a photograph in *Gold der Skythen*, p. 205)

18 'Stag-Stone.' Baikal region. Karasuk culture.
Early first millennium BC.
(After a photograph in Brentjes, Vasilievsky,
Schamanenkrone und Weltenbaum , Leipzig, 1989, ill. 15)

19 Duck and Fish on Pictish symbol stone. 1.30m high.
Easterton of Roseisle, Morayshire.

20 Twin horses with fish tails. Part (bottom right) of Pictish
cross-slab at Aberlemno churchyard (Angus).

21 Rock drawings from a grave near the Cernovaja river,
Minusinsk steppe. Early second millennium BC.
(After a photograph in M. Grjasnow, *Südsiberien* , Stuttgart,
1970, ill. 23)

22 'The Great Goddess' with wings and volute limbs.
Gold ornament from garment. 5.3cm high. Greek style,
4th century BC. From kurgan Bolschaja Blisniza,
Kuban region (Krasnodar). St. Petersburg, Hermitage.
(After a photograph in Piatrovski and others, *op. cit.*, no. 208)

23 'The Great Goddess' with snake limbs. Gold relief ornament
on horse's head-piece. 41.4cm high. Greco-Scythian style.
4th century BC. From kurgan Cimbalka, Dnieper region.
St. Petersburg, Hermitage.
(After a photograph in *Gold der Skythen* , p. 101)

24 Shrivatsa, the sign of happiness.
(E. Schleberger, *Die Indische Götterwelt* , Köln, 1986, p. 274)

25 Shrivatsa as symbol of fertility, with lotuses and fish tails.
(E. Schleberger, *ibid* , p. 274)

26 A Shrivatsa symbol for the goddess Lakshmi being bathed
by two elephants. (E. Schleberger, *ibid*, p. 276)

27 'The Great Goddess' on the Gundestrup cauldron. First half of
1st century BC. Copenhagen, Nationalmuseet.
(After a photograph in S. and P. F. Botheroyd, *Lexikon der
Keltischen Mythologie* , Munich, 1992, p. 279)

28 Indian fish symbol of happiness.
(E. Schleberger, *op. cit.*, p. 191)

29 Decoration ('crest' of the 'Great Goddess') on helmet in iron
and bronze embossing and openwork with coral studs.
From Canosa di Puglia (Bari). 23.2cm high. First half of
4th century BC. Berlin, Staatliche Museen, Antikensammlung
Preussischer Kulturbesitz.
(After a photograph in *The Celts* , *op. cit.*, p. 200)

30 'Crest' of the 'Great Goddess' on a bronze fitting in the form
    of a horse's head, from Stanwick (Yorkshire). 10.1cm high.
    First century BC. London, British Museum.
    (After a photograph in *The Celts , op. cit.*, p.27)
31 Symbol stone at the tower, Abernethy (Fife) with 'crest'
    of the 'Great Goddess' on lower part of stone.
32 'Crest' of the 'Great Goddess' on a lead disc, 50mm across,
    from the Brough of Birsay.
33 Spiral breast ornament on a bronze figurine of a seated
    fertility goddess, from Beirut. Syrian, 14th-12th centuries BC.
    16cm high. Paris, Louvre.
    (After a photograph in H. Frankfort, *The Art and
    Architecture of the Ancient Orient* , Penguin Books, 1954,
    1969, plate 144B; Yale University Press, 1970, ill. 300)
34 Two Scythians on kneeling horses. Terminals of a gold torque.
    25.8cm diam. Greco-Scythian art. 4th century BC.
    From kurgan Kul-Oba, Kertsch (Crimea). St. Petersburg,
    Hermitage.
    (After a photograph in B. Piatrovski, *op. cit.*, no. 127)
35 Pictish horseman on back of cross-slab, Meigle no. 3.
    Meigle Museum, Perth and Kinross.
36 Goddess Epona on horseback. A stele from the Rhineland.
    2nd century BC. Bonn, Rheinisches Landesmuseum.
    (After a photograph in *The Celts , op. cit.*, p. 431)
37 Pfalzfeld column, a Celtic menhir, with mistletoe foliage.
    Bonn, Rheinisches Landesmuseum.
    (After a photograph in Botheroyd, *op. cit.*, foll. p. 288)
38 Top part of a headdress, in the form of an open cylinder,
    decorated with a female figure (a fertility goddess) repeated
    four times and seated amongst flowers and plants.
    Gold. 7.7cm high. Greek. 4th century BC. From kurgan Kul-Oba
    (Crimea). St. Petersburg, Hermitage.
    (After a photograph in Piatrovski, *op. cit.*, no. 181)
39 Lions attacking horses and stags. Part of an omphalos plate
    with relief decoration. Gold. 21.8cm diam. Greco-Scythian art.
    First half of 4th century BC. From kurgan Solocha,
    Saporoshje. St. Petersburg, Hermitage.
    (After a photograph in Piatrovski, *ibid* , no. 162-3)
40 Stag resting, with dog and other creatures. A shield emblem
    with relief decoration. Gold. 16x31.5cm. Greco-Scythian art.

4th century BC. From kurgan Kul-Oba (Crimea).
St. Petersburg, Hermitage.
(After a photograph in Piatrovski, *ibid* , no. 213)

41   Lion. From a gold plate from Ziwiyeh. Old Urartian style.
First half of 7th century BC. Paris, Louvre.
(Akurgal, *op. cit.*, fig. 33, p. 64)

42   Lion. From a bronze shield from Topprakkale. Old Urartian.
Late 7th century BC. Ankara, Archaeological Museum.
(Akurgal, *ibid* , fig. 21, p. 57)

43   Lion. From a bronze quiver. Luristan. 7th century BC.
New York, Metropolitan Museum.
(Akurgal, *ibid* , fig. 34, p. 66)

44   The god Enki in the watery *abzu*, receives another god,
probably Shamash. From a cylinder seal of the Akkadian
period, found at Ur.
(Tessa Rickards in J. Black and A. Green, *Gods, Demons and
Symbols of Ancient Mesopotamia* , British Museum Press,
London, 1992, ill. 19, p. 27)

45   Gilgamesh and Enkidu killing lions. From a cylinder seal.
London, British Museum.
(After a photograph in S. H. Hooke, *Middle Eastern Mythology*,
Penguin, 1991, plate 14c)

46   The weather god, Adad, son of Enlil, standing on his beast.
From a cylinder seal of the Akkadian period.
(Tessa Rickards, *op. cit.*, ill. 89, p. 111)

47   Ishtar 'dressed to kill'. Detail of a cylinder seal of the
Neo-Assyrian period. (Tessa Rickards, *ibid* , ill. 87, p. 108)

48   Ishtar in astral aspect receiving worship. Detail, as above.
(Tessa Rickards, *ibid.*)

49   Fantastic sea creature: winged female figure, with snake-like
fishtail and horse legs. Lower end of a scabbard. Ivory.
Width 11.8cm. First half of 2nd century BC. From the
Tachti-Sangin temple, Oxus district, Tadjikistan.
(After a photograph in Catalogue *2000 Jahre Kunst am Oxus-
Fluss in Mittelasien* , Museum Rietberg, Zürich, 1989, p. 38)

50   Earrings in the form of a seated sphinx. Gold with blue
and green lacquer. 4.7cm long. Greco-Scythian art.
Second half of the 4th century BC. Crimea. Kiev,
Museum for Historical Treasures.
(After a photograph in Piatrovski, *op. cit.*, no. 245)

51 Gilgamesh. After a relief from Khorsabad. Assyrian.
    8th century BC.Paris, Louvre.
    (Cover of *Das Gilgamesch-Epos* , Reclam, Stuttgart, 1988)
52 The Pictish Cernunnos. Part of a stone frieze. Meigle no. 22.
    Meigle Museum.
53 Great Goddess with animals. Development of a steatite vase,
    from Khafaje. 3rd millennium BC. Ca 5cm high. London,
    British Museum.
    (H. Frankfort, *op. cit.*, Penguin, fig. 9; Yale, ill. 33)
54 The Master of Animals. Harness-piece. Bronze. Luristan.
    7th century BC.
    (Akurgal, *op. cit.*, fig. 35, p. 66)
55 Statue of a god, with Gilgamesh motive on base. Basalt.
    Height ca 320cm. Assyrian-Aramaic style. 9th century BC.
    From Sam'al.
    (After a photograph in E. Akurgal, *Die Kunst der Hethiter,*
    Munich, 1976, plate 127)
56 The Rhynie Man. Symbol stone found in Rhynie area
    (Gordon). 178cm high. Aberdeen, Woodhill House.
57 The Babylonian scribal god Nabû standing on a snake-dragon.
    Detail from a caste copper or bronze amuletic plaque of the
    Neo-Assyrian period.
    (Tessa Rickards, *op. cit.*, ill. 110, p. 134)
58 Indian makara, mythological water dragon.
    (E. Schleberger, *op. cit.*, p. 194)
59 Epona riding, from Alesia. Stone. Alise-Ste Reine (Côte d'Or):
    Musée Municipale.
    (After a photograph in Botheroyd, *op. cit.*, p. 104)
60 The Great Goddess on horseback. Detail of central figure of
    Hilton of Cadboll Stone. Edinburgh, Royal Museum.
    (After a photograph in J. Close-Brooks, *St. Ninian's Isle
    Treasure* , HMSO Edinburgh, 1981, plate 31)
61 Part of a design on a bronze situla from Luristan.
    7th century BC.
    (E. Akurgal, *op. cit.*, fig. 62, p. 84)
62 Triquetra on lower panel of Hilton of Cadboll Stone.
63 Rosmerta and Mercury. Stone relief. From Shakespeare Inn,
    Northgate Street, Gloucester. Gloucester City Museum.
    (After a photograph in M. Green, *Symbol & Image in Celtic
    Religious Art* , London, 1989, Fig. 22, p. 58)

64   The Migvie Stone, Aberdeen. Front.
     (J. Anderson, *Scotland in Early Christian Times* , Edinburgh, 1881, fig. 48, p. 77)

65   The same. Back (*Ibid* , fig. 49)

66   Winged genius on a door jamb, Pasargadae, Iran. Achaemenian relief.
     (H. Frankfort, *op. cit.*, Penguin, fig. 116; Yale, ill. 427)

67   Double discs on symbol stone at Aberlemno roadside (Angus).

68   Double discs on back of cross-slab from Golspie, Sutherland.

69   Diagram of the two discs linked together.

70   Lightning rod on Dunnichen symbol stone (Angus).

71   Double discs and lightning rod on symbol stone at Aberlemno roadside.

72   Double discs and lightning rod on Dunnichen symbol stone.

73   The 'bonds' of Enlil on symbol stone from Westfield Farm, Falkland. Falkland Palace Museum.

74   Incised image on stone from Tschernowaja (on the Yenisey north of Minussinsk). 130cm high. Tasmin culture, ca 3000 BC.
     (Brentjes, Vasilievsky, *Schamanenkrone und Weltenbaum* , Leipzig, 1989, p. 63)

75   Axe-head on plinth on symbol stone from Dunrobin, Sutherland. Dunrobin Castle Museum.

76   Axe-head on plinth on symbol stone at Abernethy tower (Fife).

77   Axe-head from Akhalkalaki, south-west Georgia. Ca 1200 BC. State Museum of Georgia.
     (After a photograph in D. M. Lang, *The Georgians* , London, 1966, pl. 13)

78   Axe-head, one of two found in bronze hoard from Gavel Moss, Renfrewshire.

79   Top part of Mesopotamian boundary stone of Mardukapiliddima (714 BC). Berlin Museum.
     (After a photograph in H. Frankfort, *op. cit.*, Penguin, pl. 120; Yale, ill. 229)

80   Temple and altar with Ea's goatfish, on Middle Assyrian seal impression.
     (H. Frankfort, *ibid* , Penguin, fig 24A; Yale, ill. 150A)

81   Incised mask image on stone plinth from Yenisey. 15th-11th centuries BC. (After a photograph in A. P. Okladnikow, *Der Hirsch mit dem goldenen Geweih: Vorgeschichtliche Felsbilder Siberiens* , Wiesbaden, 1972, pl. 15)

99 Two animals meeting and forming a single head on a
figurative relief slab from Ch'ing-ping hsien, Shantung,
China. Dated 114 AD. 88 x 119cm. Zürich, Rietberg Museum.
(After a photograph in O. Sirén, *Chinese Sculptures in the
von der Heydt Collection* , Zürich, ill. no. 2, p. 17)

100 Gajavrsabha, buffalo and elephant with one head.
(Schleberger, *op. cit.*, p. 194)

101 Two winged horses sharing the head of an owl, on a north
Italian Celtic situla. Este, Museo Nationale Atestino.
(After a photograph in Botheroyd, *op. cit.*, p. 270)

102 Zoomorphic junctures on two halberd blades, from Luristan.
(H. Frankfort, *op. cit.*, Penguin, fig. 107, Yale, ill. 410)

103 The Tantric rain god Vajrapani clad in a tiger's skin and
wearing the skin of an elephant slung over his shoulders,
crushing evil spirits under his feet.
(H.W. Schumann, *Buddhistische Bilderwelt* , Köln, 1986,
fig. 190, p. 205)

104 The Pictish elephant's skin on the side of Meigle no. 5
cross-slab. Meigle Museum.
In this and similar forms the elephant skin may be seen on,
for example, the stones at Meigle Museum, nos. 1 (see Plate 5)
and 4 (see fig. 182), Dunfallandy (see fig. 176), Golspie
(see fig. 179), Brodie (see Frontispiece), Shandwick,
the 'Maiden Stone' at Chapel of Garioch (Gordon) and the
'Elephant Stone' at Mortlach,
Dufftown (Moray); also in the sadly neglected Wemyss caves (Fife).

105 Mahakala on a bull, holding an outstretched elephant's skin.
From cave temple at Bezeklik, near Turfan, Chinese Turkestan
(now Xinjiang).
(A. Grünwedel, *Altbuddhistische Kultstätten in Chinesisch -
Turkistan* , Berlin, 1912, fig. 582, p. 281)

106 Fragment of a bronze pin disc from Luristan. 9.8cm diam.
First millennium BC. Paris, Louvre.
(A. Godard, *L'Art de L'Iran* , Arthaud, Paris, 1962, Fig 56)

107 Decorative plaque representing Gilgamesh holding two
winged animals. Bronze from Luristan. First millennium BC.
(A. Godard, *ibid* , Fig 25)

108 Seal impressions from Sumer, Protoliterate period, 3500-3000 BC.
(H. Frankfort, *op. cit.*, Penguin, fig. 7, B and D;
Yale, ill. 25, B and D)

109 'The Master of Wild Animals'. Top-piece of a cult object
from Luristan. Bronze. 17.6 cm high. First quarter of
first millennium BC.
(E. de Waele, *Bronzes du Luristan et d'Amlash* , no. 120
Collection Godard, Louvain, 1982, fig. 93, p. 113)

110 Horse on a bronze harness plaque. Zagros.
(After a photograph in A. Godard, *Le Trésor de Ziwiyé* ,
Haarlem, 1950, fig. 37, p. 47)

111 The god on the stag. Steatite relief from Yeniköy. 6.3cm **high**.
(O. R. Gurney, *The Hittites* , London, 1952, 1990, fig. 7, p. 113)

112 The sword or dagger god, Yazilikaya. Ca 3m high rock
carving.
(H. Frankfort, *op. cit.*, Penguin, fig. 53; Yale, ill. 265)

113 The warrior god from the King's Gate, Boghazköy.
Rock carving 198cm high.
(After photographs in E. Akurgal, *Die Kunst der Hethiter* ,
Plates 64 and 65)

114 King adoring bull. Alaja Hüyük bas relief on orthostat.
(H. Frankfort, *op. cit.*, Penguin, fig. 54; Yale, ill. 267)

115 Deer, from the town wall, Alaja Hüyük. Basalt orthostat relief,
81cm high. Ankara Museum.
(After a photograph in E. Akurgal, *op. cit.*, plate 96)

116 Queen Puduhepa holding up the sign of the triquetra in front
of the altar of the sun goddess. Part of rock relief at Fraktin
by Kayseri. Figures 130cm high.
(After a photograph in E. Akurgal, *op. cit.*, plate 101)

117 Triquetra sign on bronze brooch, Glasgow.
(J. Anderson, *op. cit.*, fig. 21, p.26)

118 A Hittite seal representing the Great Goddess, between the
weather god and the sun god, with the twin gods.
(G. Contenau, *La Civilisation des Hittites* , Paris, 1934,
fig. 19, p. 228)

119 Statue of a lion with human face, and wings (sphinx).
Bronze and stone, 16cm high. Urartu, 8-6th century BC.
St. Petersburg, Hermitage. Based on the 8th century BC
monumental stone sphinxes guarding the gateway to
Erebuni (Erewan).
(E. Akurgal, *Urartäische und Alt-Iranische Kunstzentren* ,
fig. 82, p. 96)

120 Lion on a bronze shield. Old Urartian style, first half of
     8th century BC.
     (E. Akurgal, *op. cit.*, fig. 78, p. 96)
121 Lion statue from Kayalidere, Varto. Middle Urartian style,
     685-645 BC. Ankara Museum. (E. Akurgal, *op. cit.*, fig. 30, p. 61)
122a Double lightning fork. Old and Neo-Babylonian symbol
     of the weather god.
     (Tessa Rickards, *op. cit.*, fig. 96, p. 118)
122b Hittite hieroglyphic sign for the weather god of the land of
     Hatti. From an epigraph incised in a monument to the last
     Hittite king, Suppiluliuma II.
     (E. Masson, *Le combat pour l'immortalité* , Paris, 1991,
     part of fig. 7, p. 238)
122c Hittite hieroglyphic sign for the weather god of the sky.
     From the basalt altars at Emirgazi (near Konya).
     (E. Masson, *ibid* , part of fig. 8, p. 239)
123 Little lion on a gold pectoral from Ziwiyeh. Ca 7th century BC.
     (After a photograph in A. Godard, *Le Trésor de Ziwiyé* ,
     Haarlem, 1950, fig. 33, p. 43)
124 Two confronted beasts, one with the 'M' sign, on a slab, no. 26,
     in Meigle Museum.
     (I. Henderson, *The Picts*, London, 1967, fig. 28, p. 135)
125 Bull-men supporting a winged sun disc. From Tell Halaf
     (Guzana). Orthostat relief ca 91cm high. Aleppo, Museum.
     (After a photograph in H. Frankfort, *op. cit.*, Penguin,
     plate 159A; Yale, ill. 345)
126 Striding lion from Tell Halaf (Guzana). Orthostat relief,
     basalt 150cm high. Early 1st millennium BC.
     Formerly Berlin Museum.
     (After a photograph in A. Parrot, *Nineveh and Babylon* ,
     London, 1961, plate 98A)
127 Decoration on an ivory box from Nimrud, with sphinxes.
     7cm high.
     (H. Frankfort, *op. cit.*, Penguin, fig. 92; Yale, ill. 372)
128 Pictish animal symbols:
     A slab with a single bull symbol, 69cm high, from Burghead.
     Edinburgh, Royal Museum.
     Part of a symbol stone showing a wolf. From Ardross
     (Ross and Cromarty). Inverness Museum.
     The Boar Stone at Knocknagael, near Inverness. Over 2m high.

129 Stag on cross-slab at Eassie (Angus).

130 Stag hunt, from Malatya. Syro-Hittite.
     (O. R. Gurney, *op. cit.*, fig. 18, p. 174)

131 Head of a deity in stone, from Heidelberg. Celtic,
     5th century BC. Karlsruhe, Badisches Landesmuseum.
     (After a photograph in *The Celts, op. cit.*, p. 34)

132 Bull on basalt relief from Ankara area. Assyrianising style,
     ca 700 BC. 104cm high.
     (After photographs in E. Akurgal, *Die Kunst der Hethiter*,
     plate 137, and K. Bittel, *Die Hethiter*, plate 335)

133 Seated weather god, with adorant. Relief from town walls of
     Alaja Hüjük. 14th century BC. 112cm high. Ankara.
     (After photographs in E. Akurgal, *ibid* , plate 93, and K. Bittel,
     ibid , plate 221)

134 Symbol stone from Gurness (Orkney).

135 Sacrifice of a bull, on Stone no. 7, St. Vigeans Museum.
     (See fig. 178)   (I. Henderson, *op. cit.*, fig. 31, p. 141)

136 Back of cross-slab at Kirriemuir (Angus).
     (J. Anderson, *op. cit.*, fig. 39, p. 62)

137 Goddess, with adorant, on the Inchbrayock slab.
     (I. Henderson, *op. cit.*, fig. 34b, p. 147)

138 Goddess with hanging braids, from Guzana (Tell Halaf).
     Basalt statue. 1.9m high. Early first millennium BC.
     Berlin Museum.
     (After a photograph in A. Parrot, *op. cit.*, plate 103)

139 The weather god Teshub, on a relief from the southern gate
     of the citadel of Zinjirli (Sam'al). Berlin Museum.
     (C. W. Ceram, *Narrow Pass, Black Mountain*,
     London, 1956, p. 39)

140 Ishtar-Tanit and double disc symbol on a stele from Dougga,
     near Carthage.
     (After a photograph in the *New Larousse Encyclopaedia of
     Mythology*, London, 1968, p. 84)

141 King Katuwas on an orthostat relief from Carchemish.
     Basalt 128.5cm high. 850-700 BC. Ankara.
     (After a photograph in E. Akurgal, *op. cit.*, plate 118)

142 Goddess Kubaba on a fragment of a relief from Carchemish.
     Basalt 82cm high. 1050-850 BC. Ankara.
     (After a photograph in E. Akurgal, *ibid* , plate 115)

143a Bracelet from the second city of Hissarlik (Troy). 2cm high.
 (H. Frankfort, *op. cit.*, Penguin, fig. 44(D); Yale, ill. 235(D)
143b Spiral patterns on a metal belt, from Boghazköy.
 (H. Frankfort, *ibid*, Penguin, fig. 58; Yale, ill. 275)
144 The archers on (a) the back of the St. Vigeans no. 1 cross-slab,
 and (b) the west face of the Shandwick cross-slab.
145 One side of a carved ivory rod, from Megiddo. 19cm high.
 Possibly 14th century BC.
 (H. Frankfort, *ibid*, Penguin, fig. 72; Yale, ill. 313)
146 Archer hunting boar and stag, on orthostat relief from the
 townwall of Alaja Hüyük. 14th-13th century BC.
 Basalt 131cm high. Ankara.
 (After a photograph in E. Akurgal, *op. cit.*, plate 94)
147 Top section of the back of the cross-slab from Aldbar
 (now in Brechin Cathedral, Angus)
148 Goddess Kubaba, enthroned on the back of a lion, on an
 orthostat relief at Carchemish. 9th century BC. Ankara.
 (After a photograph in K. Bittel, *op. cit.*, plate 289)
149 Lady and scribe on grave stele from Marash.
 Basalt. 105cm high. End 8th/early 7th century BC. Adana.
 (After a photograph in E. Akurgal, *op. cit.*, plate 138)
150 Sculpture of a seated divine or royal couple, from Guzana.
 Early first millennium BC. Basalt, 80cm high. Aleppo Museum.
 (After a photograph in A. Parrot, *op.cit.*, plate 101)
151 Mother suckling child, from west row of orthostats on
 north gate at Karatepe. Ca 700 BC.
 (After a photograph in E. Akurgal, *op. cit.*, plate 150)
152 Hero with two lions and, above, two birds attacking a prone
 deer or goat. From same row of orthostats as Fig. 151, at Karatepe.
 (After a photograph in E. Akurgal, *ibid*, plate 146)
153 Trees of Life on an embroidered tunic of Assurnasirpal,
 on a relief, from Nimrud. Ca 850 BC.
 (H. Frankfort, *op. cit.*, Penguin, fig. 41; Yale, ill. 224)
154 Tree of Life, flanked by two goats, on an orthostat relief at the
 north gate at Karatepe. End of 8th century BC.
 (After a photograph in K. Bittel, *op. cit.*, plate 311)
155 Mitannian seal impression, with stylized Tree of Life.
 Ca 1400 BC.
 (H. Frankfort, *op. cit.*, Penguin, fig. 63; Yale, ill.287)

156 Tree of Life, flanked by two deities, on a relief from
Sakjegözü. Ca 700 BC.
(H. Frankfort, *ibid* , Penguin, fig. 89; Yale, ill. 354)

157 Great Goddess holding Tree of Life. Detail from felt appliqué
tent material. Altai, Pazyryk, kurgan V. 5-4th century BC.
St. Petersburg, Hermitage.
(After a photograph in M. Grjasnow, *Südsiberien* ,
Stuttgart, 1970, plate 136)

158 Centaur carrying a tree, on a Phrygian pottery plaque from
Pazarli. Ankara.
(After a photograph in K. Akurgal, *Phrygische Kunst* ,
Ankara 1955, plate 49b)

159 Stele from church at Gaiana, Armenia. Carved stone.
9-10th century AD. (After a photograph in T. Talbot Rice,
Ancient Arts of Central Asia , London, 1965, ill. 212, p. 229)

160 Stele from Etshmiadsin, near Erewan. Carved stone.
11-12th century AD.
(After a photogaph in U. Bock, *Georgien und Armenien* ,
Köln, 1988, plate 28)

161 Column capital at Kutais cathedral, Georgia. Early 12th century AD.
(After a photograph in T. Talbot Rice, *op. cit.*, ill. 231, p. 245)

162 An inside panel of the Gundestrup bowl, showing a sacrificial
scene with a procession of warriors and musicians.
Embossed silver plaque. First half of 1st century BC.
Copenhagen, Nationalmuseet.
(After a photograph in J. P. Mallory, *op. cit.*, plate 20)

163 One side of a silver chape from a sword scabbard. One of two
from the treasure hoard found on St. Ninian's Isle in Shetland.
8.2cm wide. Ca 8th century AD. Edinburgh, Royal Museum.
(After a photograph in J. Close-Brooks, *St. Ninian's Isle
Treasure*, Edinburgh, 1981, ill. 16)

164 Detail of a picture-stone from Tjängvide, Gotland, Sweden.
9th century AD.
(O. Klindt-Jensen, *The World of the Vikings* ,
New York, 1970, p. 210)

165 'Ribbon-animals' in the Jellinge style, named after the
decoration on a small silver cup from a royal grave at Jelling,
Jutland, Denmark. Ca 850-1000 AD.
(O. Klindt-Jensen, *ibid* , p. 198)

166 The pointed symbol stone, Clach Biorach, at Edderton (Easter Ross).

167 Gold plaque of Bee Goddess from Camiros, Rhodes.
7th century BC. Boston, Museum of Fine Arts.
(After a photograph in M. Gimbutas, *The Gods and Goddesses of Old Europe* , London, 1974, plate 179)

168 Painted representation of goddess with wings in the shape of a double-axe (resembling a butterfly) on a floral stem.
Late Minoan I, island of Mochlos, Crete.
(M. Gimbutas, *ibid* , fig. 153, p. 187, and A. B. Cook, *Zeus a Study in Ancient Religion* , vol. II, Cambridge, 1940, fig. 395)

169 The weather god fighting the snake-dragon of Chaos.
Stone relief from Malatya. 10th century BC.
(E. Masson, *Le combat pour l'immortalité* , Paris, 1991, Fig. 2, p. 51)

170 Pairs of snakes and snake-dragon flanking the cross on the St. Vigeans no. 1 cross-slab. (Detail).
St. Vigeans Museum (Angus).

171 Steatite cover of a lamp or dish with coiled snakes.
Ca 7cm wide. Neo-Sumerian period, ca 2125-2025 BC.
(After a photograph in H. Frankfort, *op. cit.*, Penguin, plate 51C; Yale, ill. 102)

172 Votive stones with snake motifs. Indian.
(E. Schleberger, *op. cit.*, drawings on p. 182)

173 Front of cross-slab at Glamis Manse (Angus). 270cm high.

174 Back of cross-slab at Cossans (Angus). 'St. Orland's Stone'.
Ca 280cm high. Probably on its original site.

175 Back of cross-slab in Aberlemno churchyard (Angus).

176 Front of cross-slab, Dunfallandy. 146cm high.
At Dunfallandy cottage, near Pitlochry (Perth and Kinross).

177 Back of cross-slab, Dunfallandy.

178 Front of cross-slab, St. Vigeans no. 7.
St. Vigeans (Angus) Museum.

179 Back of cross-slab from Golspie (Sutherland). 270cm high.
Dunrobin Castle Museum.

180 Back of cross-slab, Meigle no. 4.

181 Front of cross-slab, Meigle no. 4. Meigle Museum (Angus).

182 Front of slab from Murthly (Perth and Kinross). Decorated on one side only. 113cm long. Edinburgh, Royal Museum.

183 Fragments of front of slab from Brough of Birsay (Orkney).
Fragments re-assembled and restored. 187cm high.
Edinburgh, Royal Museum.

SELECT BIBLIOGRAPHY

AKURGAL, E., *Phrygische Kunst* , Türk Tarih Kurumu Basimevi,
Ankara, 1955

AKURGAL, E., *Urartäische und Altiranische Kunstzentren* , Türk
Tarih Kurumu Basimevi, Ankara, 1968

AKURGAL, E. and M. HIRMER, *Die Kunst der Hethiter* , Hirmer Verlag,
Munich, 1961, 1976

ALLEN, J. R. , *Celtic Art in Pagan and Christian Times* , London, 1904,
facsimile edition, Studio Editions, London, 1993

ALLEN, J. R. and J. ANDERSON, *The early Christian monuments of
Scotland* , Edinburgh, 1903, Reprinted by Pinkfoot Press, 1993

ANDERSON, J., *Scotland in early Christian times* , (second series)
David Douglas, Edinburgh, 1881

BASILOV, V. N. and others, *Nomads of Central Asia* (trans. from
Russian), National History Museum of Los Angeles and
University of Washington Press, 1989

BEDE, *Ecclesiastical History of the English People* (trans. by
L. Sherley-Price), Penguin Books, London, 1955, 1968, 1990

BITTEL, K., *Die Hethiter* , Verlag C. H. Beck, Munich, 1976

BLACK, J. and A. GREEN, *Gods , Demons and Symbols of Ancient
Mesopotamia* , British Museum Press, London, 1992

BLURTON, T.R., *Hindu Art* , British Museum Press, London, 1992

BOARDMAN, J., *Pre-Classical , From Crete to Archaic Greece* ,
Penguin, London, 1967

BOCK, U., *Georgien und Armenien*, DuMont, Köln, 1988

BOTHEROYD, S. and P. F., *Lexikon der Keltischen Mythologie* ,
Diederichs Verlag, Munich, 1992

BRENTJES, B. and R. S. VASILIEVSKY, *Schamanenkrone und Weltenbaum:
Kunst der Nomaden Nordasiens* (trans. from Russian), VEB E. A.
Seeman Verlag, Leipzig, 1989

BRØNSTEDT, J., *Nordische Vorzeit* , Band 2, Bronzezeit in Dänemark,
and Band 3, Eisenzeit in Dänemark, Karl Wachholz Verlag,
Neumünster, 1962 and 1963

BURKART-BAUER, M-F., *Chinesische Jaden* , Museum Rietberg,
Zürich, 1986

CAMPBELL, J., E. JOHN and P. WORMALD, *The Anglo-Saxons* , Penguin,
London, (1982), 1991

CERAM, C.W., *Gods , Graves and Scholars* , Hamburg, 1949, Gollancz,
London, 1952

CERAM, C. W., *Narrow Pass , Black Mountain* , Hamburg, 1955, Gollancz,
London, 1956

CHADWICK, N., *The Celts* , Penguin, London, 1971, reprinted 1991

CLOSE-BROOKS, J., *St . Ninian's Isle Treasure* , HMSO, Edinburgh, 1981

CLOSE-BROOKS, J. and R. B. K. STEVENSON, *Dark Age Sculpture* , HMSO, Edinburgh, 1982

CONTENAU, G., *La Civilisation des Hittites et des Mitanniens* , Payot, Paris,1934

CRAVEN, R. A., *A concise history of Indian Art* , Thames and Hudson, London, 1976, reprinted 1991

DALLEY, S., *Myths from Mesopotamia* , Oxford University Press, 1989

DAVIDSON, H. R. E., *Myths and symbols in pagan Europe : early Scandinavian and Celtic religions* , Manchester University Press,1988

DEYDIER, C., *Les Bronzes chinois* , Office du Livre, Fribourg, 1980

DUMÉZIL, G., *Légendes sur les Nartes* , Librairie Champion, Paris, 1930

DUMÉZIL, G., *L'idéologie tripartie des Indo-Européens* , Latomus, Brussels, 1958

DUMÉZIL, G., *Mythe et épopée I : L'idéologie des trois fonctions dans les épopées des peuples indo-européens* , Gallimard, Paris, 1968,1986

DUMÉZIL, G., *Les dieux souverains des Indo-Européens*, Gallimard, Paris,1977, 1980

DUVAL, P-M., *Les Celtes* , Gallimard, Paris, 1977

ELIADE, M., *Images and symbols* , Princeton University Press, (1952), 1991. (trans. from French).

ELIADE, M., *Shamanism : Archaic techniques of ecstasy* , Penguin Arkana, London, (1964), 1989. (from French).

ESSEN, G-W. and T. T. THINGO, *Die Götter des Himalaya : Buddhistische Kunst Tibets* (2 vol. exhibition catalogue Cologne, Munich, Berlin, 1989/90), Prestel Verlag, Munich, 1989

FITZGERALD, C. P., *China : a short cultural history* , The Cresset Library, London, 1986

FOX, C., *Pattern and Purpose : a survey of early Celtic Art in Britain* , National Museum of Wales, Cardiff, 1958

FRANK, I. M. and D. M. BROWNSTONE, *The Silk Road : a history* , Facts On File Publications, New York, 1986

FRANKFORT, H., *The Art and Architecture of the Ancient Orient* , Penguin, London, 1954, 1969, Yale University Press, 1970

GANTZ, J., *Early Irish Myths and Sagas* , Penguin, London, 1981

GARELLI, P. (Ed.), *Gilgames et sa légende* , Cahiers du Groupe F-T-D-1, Paris, 1960

GEOFFREY of Monmouth, *The History of the Kings of England* , (trans. L. Thorpe), Penguin, London, 1966

GHIRSHMAN, R., *Persia: From the origins to Alexander the Great*, Thames and Hudson, London, 1964 (from French)

GHIRSHMAN, R., *Iran: Parthians and Sassanians*, Thames and Hudson, London,1962, (from French)

GIMBUTAS, M., *Bronze Age Cultures in Central and Eastern Europe* ,
Mouton & Co., The Hague, 1965

GIMBUTAS, M., *The Gods and Goddesses of Old Europe* , 7000-3500 BC,
Thames and Hudson, London, 1974

GODARD, A., *Bronzes du Luristan* , Editions G. van Oest, Paris, 1931

GODARD, A., *Le Trésor de Ziwiyè* , Joh. Enschedé en Zonen,
Haarlem, 1950

GODARD, A., *L'Art de l'Iran* , Arthaud, Paris, 1962. English edition:
The Art of Iran, Allen & Unwin, London, 1965

GOMBOS, K. and K. GINK, *Die Baukunst Armeniens* , Genesis Verlag,
Balzers, 1973. (from Hungarian).

GOVINDA, Lama A., *Psycho - cosmic Symbolism of the Buddhist Stupa* ,
Dharma Publishing, California, 1976

GREEN, M., *Symbol & Image in Celtic Religious Art* , Routledge,
London, 1989

GRJASNOW, M., *Südsiberian* , Archaeologia Mundi, Nagel,
Stuttgart, 1970. (from Russian).

GRÜNWEDEL, A., *Altbuddhistische Kultstätten in Chinesisch-
Turkistan* , G. Reimer Verlag, Berlin, 1912

GRÜNWEDEL, A., *Alt-Kutscha* , O. Elsner Verlag, Berlin, 1920

GURNEY, O. R., *The Hittites* , Penguin, London, 1952, 1954,
reprinted 1981, 1990

HENDERSON, I., *The Picts* , Thames and Hudson, London, 1967

HERODOTUS, *The Histories* , Book IV, transl. by A. de Selincourt, rev.
by A. R. Burn, Penguin, London, 1972

HERRMANN, G., 'The Sassanian Rock Reliefs at Bishapur,'
in *Iranische Denkmäler* , Deutsches Archaeologisches Institut,
Teheran, Vols. 9 and 10, 1980 and 1981

HOOKE, S. H. (Ed.), *Myth and Ritual* , Oxford University Press,
London, 1933

HOOKE, S. H., *Babylonian and Assyrian Religion* , Hutchinson, 1953

HOOKE, S. H., *Middle East Mythology* , Penguin, London, 1963,
reprinted 1991

JACOBSTHAL, P. F., *Early Celtic Art* , 2 vols., Oxford University Press,
1944, reprinted 1969

JAMES, E. O., *Myth and Ritual in the Ancient Near East* ,
Thames and Hudson, London, 1958

JAMES, E. O., *The Ancient Gods* , Weidenfeld and Nicholson,
London, 1960

KARABELNIK, M. (Ed), *Aus den Schatzkammern Eurasiens —
Meisterwerke Antiker Kunst* , Catalogue of Exhibition at
Kunsthaus, Zürich, 1993

KLINDT-JENSEN, O., *The World of the Vikings* , Robert B. Luce Inc.,
Washington-New York, 1970

KOHL, J. G., *Reisen in Südrussland* , Dresden and Leipzig, 1841

LANG, D.M., *The Georgians* , Thames and Hudson, London, 1966

LE COQ, A. von, *Die Buddhistische Spätantike in Mittelasien* , Verlag D.
Riemer and E. Vohsen, Berlin, Part 3 Die Wandmalerei, 1924,
Parts 5, 1926, 6, 1928 and 7, 1933, Neue Bildwerke I, II, III.

LE COQ, A. von, *Chotscho* , D. Riemer Verlag, Berlin, 1913

LEROI-GOURHAN, A., *Les religions de la préhistoire , Paléolithique* ,
Presses Universitaires de France, 1964, 1971

LITTLETON, C. S., *The New Comparative Mythology* , University of
California Press, Berkeley, 1966, 1973, 1982

MACEOIN, G. S., 'On the Irish Legend of the Origin of the Picts', *Studia
Hibernica* No. 4, Dublin, 1964, pp. 138-154

MACKIE, J. D., *A History of Scotland* , Penguin, London, 1964, 1978

MACNEILL, E., 'The Language of the Picts', *Yorkshire Celtic Studies* ,
Leeds, 1938-9, pp. 3-45

MACQUEEN, J. G., *The Hittites and their Contemporaries in Asia Minor*,
Thames and Hudson, London, 1975, 1986

MALLORY, J. P., *In Search of the Indo-Europeans : Language ,
Archaeology and Myth* , Thames and Hudson, London, 1989,
reprinted 1992

MASSON, E., *Le combat pour l'immortalité : Héritage indo-européen
dans la mythologie anatolienne* , Presses Universitaires de
France, Paris, 1991

MERHART, G. von, *Bronzezeit am Jenissei* , Anton Schroll, Vienna, 1926

METTLER, M. L., *Atmosphärische Reizstreifen : Das Mass-System
antiker Völker* , Moser Verlag, Zürich, 1986

MICHELL, G., L. LEACH and T. S. MAXWELL, *In the Image of Man :
the Indian perception of the Universe through 2000 years of
painting and sculpture* , Arts Council exhibition,
Weidenfeld & Nicholson, London, 1982

MOORE, G., *Ancient Pillar Stones of Scotland* , Edinburgh, 1865

MOORTGAT, A., *The Art of Ancient Mesopotamia* , Phaidon, London,
1969. (from German, Dumont, Cologne, 1967, 1982).

NERSESSIAN, S der, *Armenian Art* , Thames and Hudson, London, 1978

NERSESSIAN, S der, *The Armenians* , Thames and Hudson, London, 1969

NEW LAROUSSE ENCYCLOPAEDIA OF MYTHOLOGY, Hamlyn,
London, 1968

O'FLAHERTY, W. D., *The Rig Veda : An Anthology* , Penguin,
London, 1981

OKLADNIKOW, A. P., *Der Hirsch mit dem goldenen Geweih :
Vorgeschichtliche Felsbilder Siberiens* , (from Russian),
Brockhaus, Wiesbaden, 1972

OVID, *Metamorphoses* , trans. by M. M. Innes, Penguin, London, 1955

PARROT, A., *Nineveh and Babylon* , Thames and Hudson, London, 1961. (from French).

PIOTROWSKI, B., *Urartu* , Archaelogia Mundi, Nagel Verlag, Munich, 1969. (from Russian).

PIOTROWSKI, B. and others, *Gold der Skythen aus der Leningrader Hermitage* , Staatlichen Antikensammlungen, Munich, 1984

PIOTROWSKI, B., L. GALANINA and N. GRATSCH, *Skythian Art* , Aurora Art, Leningrad, and Phaidon, London, 1987

PRITCHARD, J. B. (Ed.), *Ancient Near Eastern Texts Relating to the Old Testament* , Princeton University Press, 1955, 1969

PRITCHARD, J. B. (Ed.), *The Ancient Near East in Pictures Relating to the Old Testament* , Princeton UP, 1954, 1970

PRITCHARD, J. B. (Ed.), *The Ancient Near East : Supplementary Text and Pictures Relating to the Old Testament* , Princeton UP, 1969

RANKIN, F., *The Wemyss Caves* , Wemyss Environmental Education Centre, Fife.

RCAHMS, *Pictish Symbol Stones, A Handlist,* Royal Commission on the Ancient and Historical Monuments of Scotland, Edinburgh, 1994

READE, J., *Mesopotamia* , British Museum Press, London, 1991

RENFREW, C., *Archaeology and Language : the puzzle of Indo-European origins* , Penguin, London, 1987, 1989

RHYS, J., *Early Ethnology of the British Isles* , The Rhind Lectures in Archaeology 1889, Society of Antiquaries of Scotland.

RICHTER, G. M. A., *A Handbook of Greek Art* , Phaidon, London, 1959, 1987 (9th edition), reprinted 1992

RICKENBACH, J. (Ed.), and S. BONADURER, *2000 Jahre Kunst am Oxus-Fluss in Mittelasien* , Museum Rietberg, Zürich, 1989

RITCHIE, A., *Picts* , HMSO, Edinburgh, 1989, reprinted 1993

ROLLE, R., *Die Welt der Skythen* , Verlag Bucher, Frankfurt, 1980. American edition: *The World of the Skythians* , Berkeley and Los Angeles, 1989

RUBRUK, W. von, *Reisen zum Grosskhan der Mongolen von Konstantinopel nach Karakorum 1253-55* , (Ed. H. D. Leicht), Thienemann, Stuttgart, 1984

RUDENKO, S. I., *Frozen Tombs of Siberia : the Pazyryk Burials of Iron Age Horsemen* , (trans. from Russian and preface by M. W. Thompson), Dent, London, 1970

SANDERS, N. K., *The Epic of Gilgamesh* , (trans.), Penguin, London, 1960, 1972

SANDERS, N. K., *Prehistoric Art in Europe* , Penguin, London, 1968, 1985

SARKISSIAN, K., *The Council of Chalcedon and the Armenian Church* , S. P. C. K., London, 1965

SCHLEBERGER, E., *Die Indische Götterwelt* , Diederichs Verlag,
    Köln, 1986

SCHOTT, A. (trans.) and W. von SODEN (Ed.), *Das Gilgamesch-Epos* ,
    Reclam, Stuttgart, 1958, 1988

SCHUMANN, H. W., *Buddhistische Bilderwelt* , Diederichs, Köln, 1986

SEIDL, U., 'Die Elamische Felsreliefs von Kurangun und Naqs-E
    Rustam,' in *Iranische Denkmäler* , Deutsches Archaeologisches
    Institut, Teheran, Vol. 12, 1986

SIKOJEV, A., *Die Narten* , *Söhne der Sonne : Mythen und Heldensagen
    der Skythen , Sammaten und Osseten* , Diederichs, Köln, 1985

SIREN, O., *Chinese Sculptures in the von der Heydt collection* ,
    Museum Rietberg, Zürich, 1959

STEAD, I. M., *Celtic Art* , British Museum, London, 1989

STENBERGER, M., *Vorgeschichte Schwedens, Nordische Vorzeit* , Band 4,
    Wachholtz Verlag, Neumünster, 1977

STOLZ, A., *Schamanen - Ekstase und Jenseitssymbolik* , DuMont,
    Köln, 1988

STROMMENGER, E., *The Art of Ancient Mesopotamia* , Thames and Hudson,
    London, 1964. (from German, Hirmer, 1962)

STRZYGOWSKI, J., *Altai-Iran und Völkerwanderung* , Leipzig, 1917

STRZYGOWSKI, J., *Die Baukunst der Armenier und Europa* , 2 vols.,
    A. Schroll, Vienna, 1918

STUART, J., *Sculptured Stones of Scotland* , 2 vols., Vol. 1, Aberdeen,
    1856, Vol. 2, Edinburgh, 1867

SUTHERLAND, E., *In Search of the Picts* , Constable, London, 1994

TALBOT RICE, T., *The Scythians* , Thames and Hudson, London, 1957

TALBOT RICE, T., *Ancient Arts of Central Asia* , Thames and Hudson,
    London, 1965

TRÜMPELMANN, L. von, 'Das Sasanidische Felsrelief von Darab',
    in *Iranische Denkmäler* , Deutsches Archaeologisches Institut,
    Teheran, Vol. 6, 1975

VENICE, Palazzo Grassi Exhibition catalogue and essays,
    The Celts , the origins of Europe , Bompiani, Milan, 1991

VENICE, Palazzo Grassi Exhibition catalogue and essays,
    The Phoenicians , Bompiani, Milan, 1988

WAELE, E. de, *Bronzes du Luristan et d'Amlash* ,
    Ancienne Collection Godard, Louvain-La-Neuve, 1982

WAINWRIGHT F. T. (Ed.), *The Problem of the Picts* , especially
    Chap. 1, 'The Picts and the problem' by F. T. Wainwright,
    Chap. 5, 'Pictish Art' by R. B. K. Stevenson, and
    Chap. 6, 'The Pictish Language' by K. H. Jackson.
    Nelson, London, 1955, reprint Melven Press, Perth, 1980

WALDSCHMIDT, E., *Gandhara — Kutscha — Turfan* ,
    Klinkhardt & Biermann Verlag, Leipzig, 1925

WALLACE-HADRILL, J. M., *Bede's Ecclesiastical History of the English People — a historical commentary* , Clarendon, Oxford, 1988

WATSON, W., *Cultural frontiers in Ancient East Asia* , Edinburgh University Press, 1971

WEBSTER, L. and J. BACKHOUSE (Eds.), *The Making of England : Anglo-Saxon Art and Culture AD 600-900* , Exhibition catalogue, British Museum, London, 1991

WHITFIELD, R. (Ed.),R. GOEPPER and others, *Treasures from Korea* , Exhibition catalogue, British Museum, London, 1984

WILSON, D. M., *Anglo-Saxon Art* , Thames and Hudson, London, 1984

WILSON, D. M., *The Vikings and their origins* , Thames and Hudson, London, 1989

YOUNGS, S. (Ed.), *The Work of Angels : Masterpieces of Celtic Metalwork 6th -9th centuries AD* , Exhibition catalogue, British Museum, London, 1989

ZIMMER, H., 'Matriarchy among the Picts', in *Leabhar nan Gleann* by G. Henderson, Edinburgh, 1898, pp. 1-42

ZIMMER, H., *Spiel um den Elefanten* , Diederichs, Köln, (1929), 1976

ZIMMER, H., *Myths and Symbols in Indian Art and Civilization* , New York, 1946, Princeton, 1974

INDEX
(Figures in brackets refer to illustrations)

258

* * *

NOTE

For the sake of clarity, the diacritical
marks commonly used to indicate the
particular sounds of certain Indian
letters have been omitted.

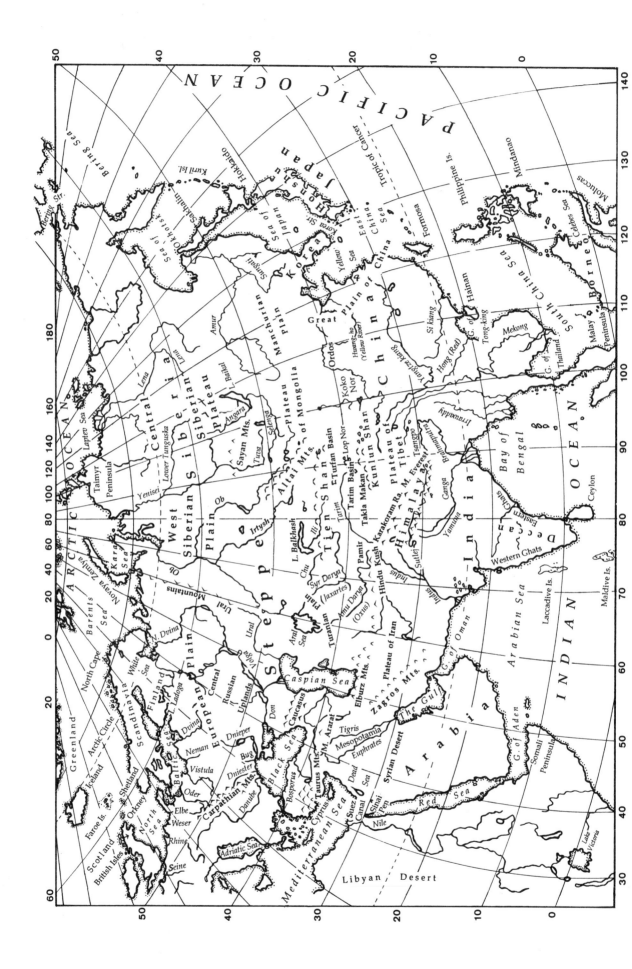